Fuck Your 9-5!
An Adult Coloring Book for People Who Hate Their Jobs and/or Boss

Author: Anthony Lee
Published in 2023

Cover and Illustrations: Our Lord and Savior Cthulhu

For information on rights and permissions, please contact:

AnthonyLeeLMFT@outlook.com

About the Author

Therapist, Artist, and Author

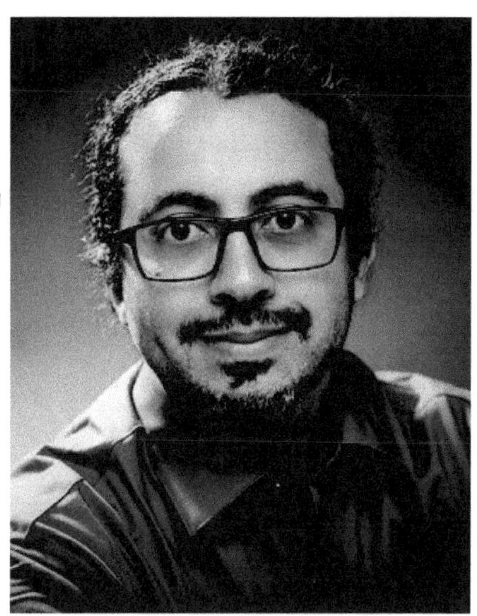

Anthony Lee is not your typical author. As a Licensed Marriage & Family Therapist, he has spent years navigating the intricate landscapes of human relationships, helping people find their way through life's complexities. His journey to creating this adult coloring book was inspired by a unique blend of professional experience and creative expression.

From Therapist to Illustrator

Anthony's professional background, which includes both private and public sector work, exposed him to the myriad challenges of the modern workplace. Dealing with bosses, coworkers, and office politics can be both hilarious and infuriating. Drawing from his own experiences, Anthony decided to channel his creativity into a different medium.

Finding Humor in Chaos

The inspiration for this coloring book came from the encounters with those bosses we all love to hate. Anthony wanted to provide readers with a humorous escape from the daily trials of terrible bosses, difficult coworkers, and the general absurdity of office life. In his pages, you'll find a unique blend of dark and light humor, reflecting the highs and lows of the working world.

Artistic Exploration

While Anthony may not have formal training in art, he brings his vision to life through sketches, descriptions, and the magic of AI art. His creations capture the essence of common office struggles, offering readers a delightful and cathartic coloring experience.

The Message

Behind the humor, there's a deeper message. Anthony's coloring book reminds us that work is just a part of life, and even the worst situations can be overcome. It encourages readers to find the silver linings, laugh at the chaos, and stand up to workplace bullies. The book serves as a reminder that together, we can navigate the treacherous waters of office politics and emerge stronger.

Personal Favorites

Two pages in particular hold special significance for Anthony. "Bosszilla Attacks" vividly illustrates the chaos that toxic bosses can unleash, while "Satan's Self-Care" humorously exposes the absurdity of those who preach positivity while creating a negative work environment.

Beyond the Book

Outside the world of art and therapy, Anthony is a passionate fan of superhero stories, exploring the intersections of psychology and relationships in these captivating narratives.

With his unique blend of creativity and professional insight, Anthony Lee invites you to join him on a coloring journey through the hilarity and challenges of office life.

Welcome to "Fuck Your 9-5!"

Thank you for picking up "Fuck Your 9-5!" An Adult Coloring Book for People Who Hate Their Job and/or Boss. I'm absolutely thrilled that you've chosen to embark on this colorful journey with me. Your presence here means the world, and I can't wait for you to dive into this unique coloring experience.

Discovering the Comedy in Chaos

Work can be a wild rollercoaster filled with ups, downs, and loop-de-loops. In this coloring book, we'll navigate the insanity of office life together and discover the humor hidden beneath the chaos. Through intricate designs and witty illustrations, you'll have the opportunity to bring your own splash of color to the absurdity of the 9-to-5 grind.

Stress Relief and Creative Focus

Coloring isn't just a fun pastime; it's a powerful stress-relief tool. You're invited to bring this book to meetings, conferences, or any situation that requires your attention. As your hands stay busy with vibrant shades, you can quietly tune into the work conversation while letting your creative side flow freely in the background. It's a clever way to maintain your focus and sanity amidst the daily grind.

Your Personal Canvas

Each page in this coloring book is your canvas, a chance to infuse your own perspective and style into the world of work. Experiment with different color schemes, try out new techniques, and embrace your inner artist. It's all about making "Fuck Your 9-5!" uniquely yours.

Acknowledgments

I'd like to express my gratitude to the terrible bosses who unwittingly provided the lemons for me to squeeze into this book. Their antics were a wellspring of inspiration. I also want to extend a heartfelt thank you to my incredible wife, Jessica, for her unwavering support and encouragement throughout this creative endeavor. Lastly, to my work spouses, Jamie and Josh, who helped me see the ridiculousness and chaos in the trenches – your camaraderie was invaluable.

Connect with Me

If you'd like to share your coloring journey or simply stay updated on my artistic escapades, you can find me on Instagram: @AnthonyLeeLMFT.

Once again, thank you for choosing "Fuck Your 9-5!" Enjoy the escape, embrace the humor, and, most importantly, let's have a blast coloring our way through the madness of the working world!

Warmly,

Anthony

The Monday Blues

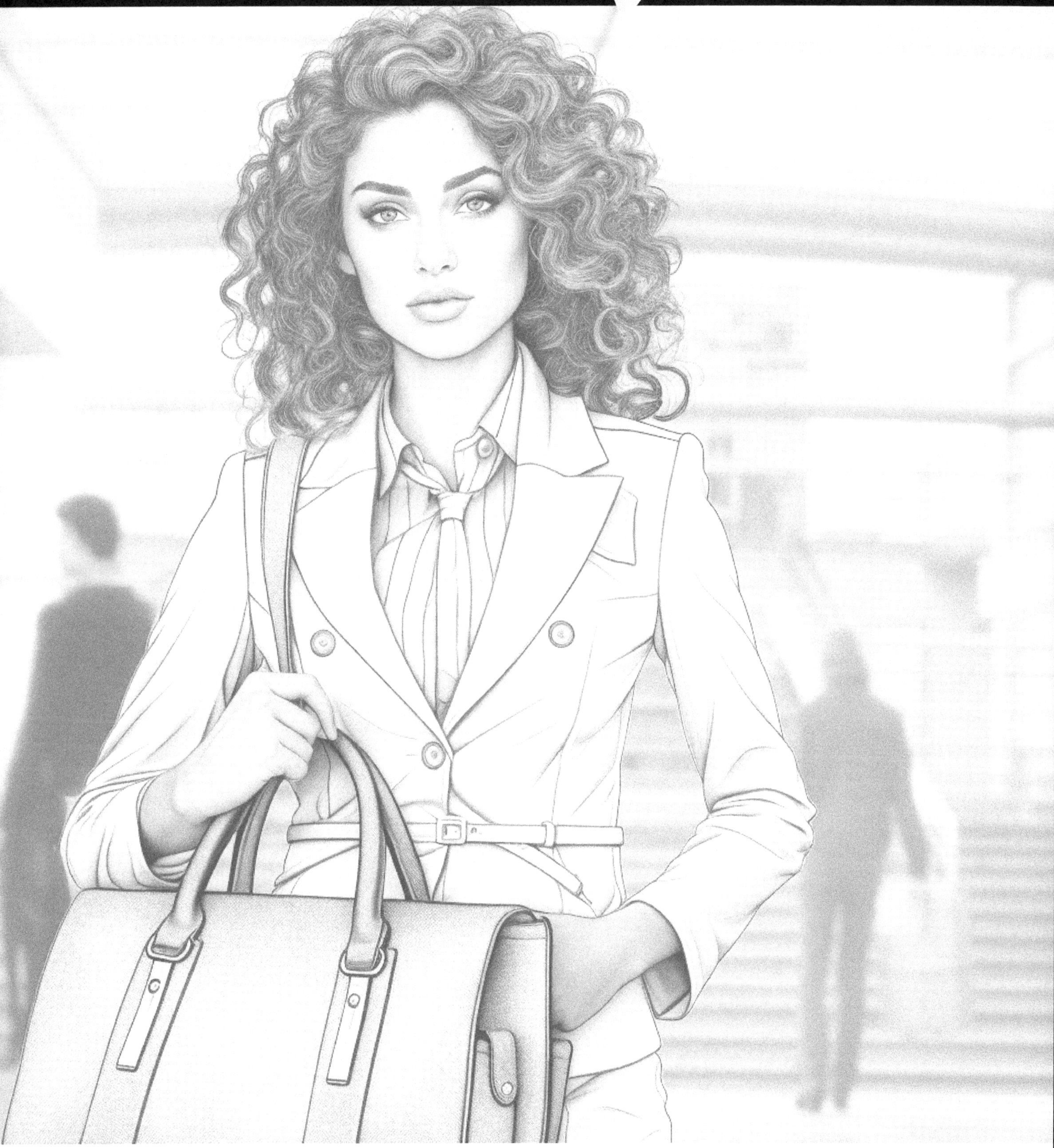

When your weekend felt shorter than a one-sentence email.

Googlenauts

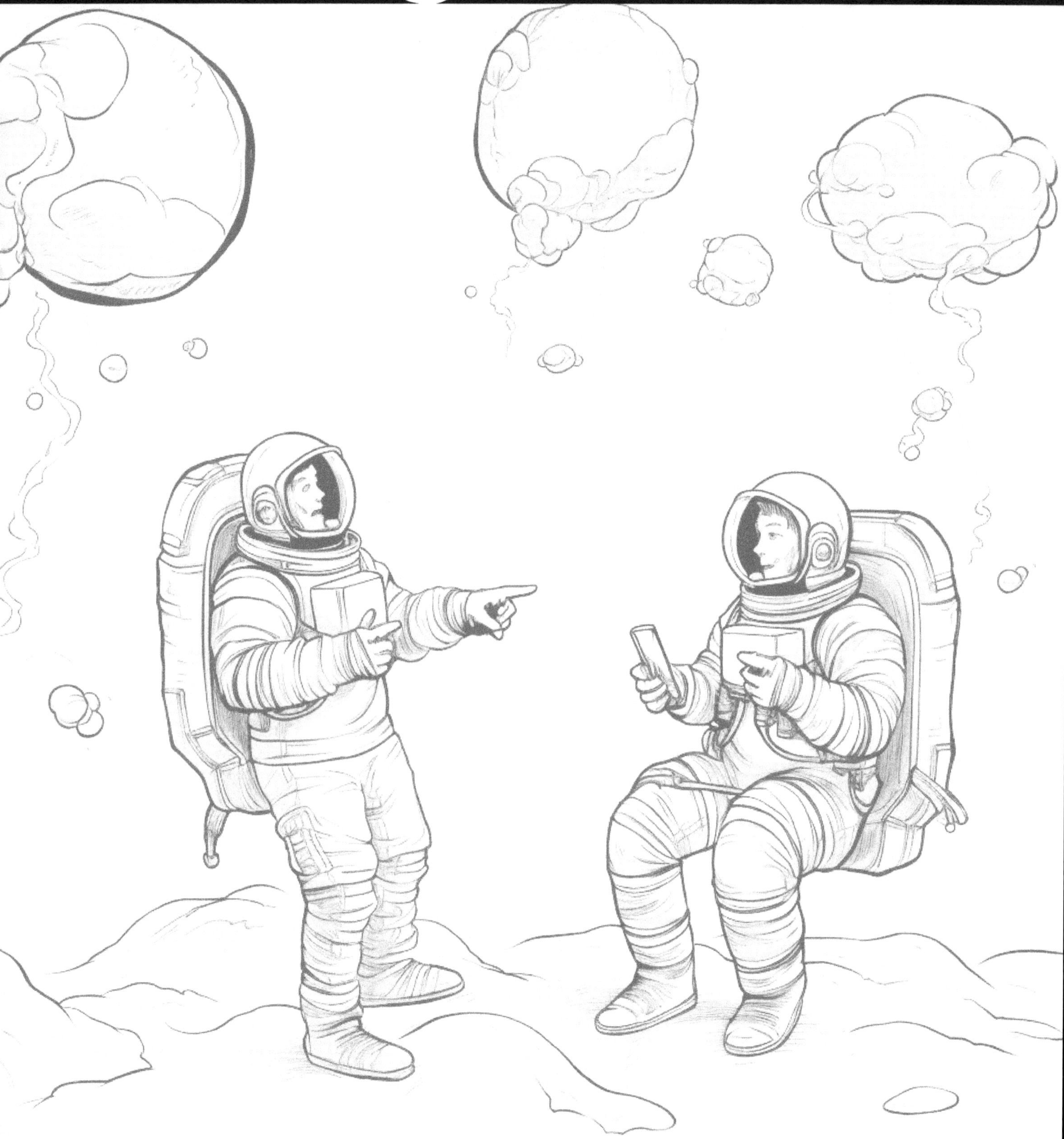

Witness the daring mission of the Googlenauts, as they journey through the cosmos asking questions that are light-years beyond Google's reach.

Groundhog Desk

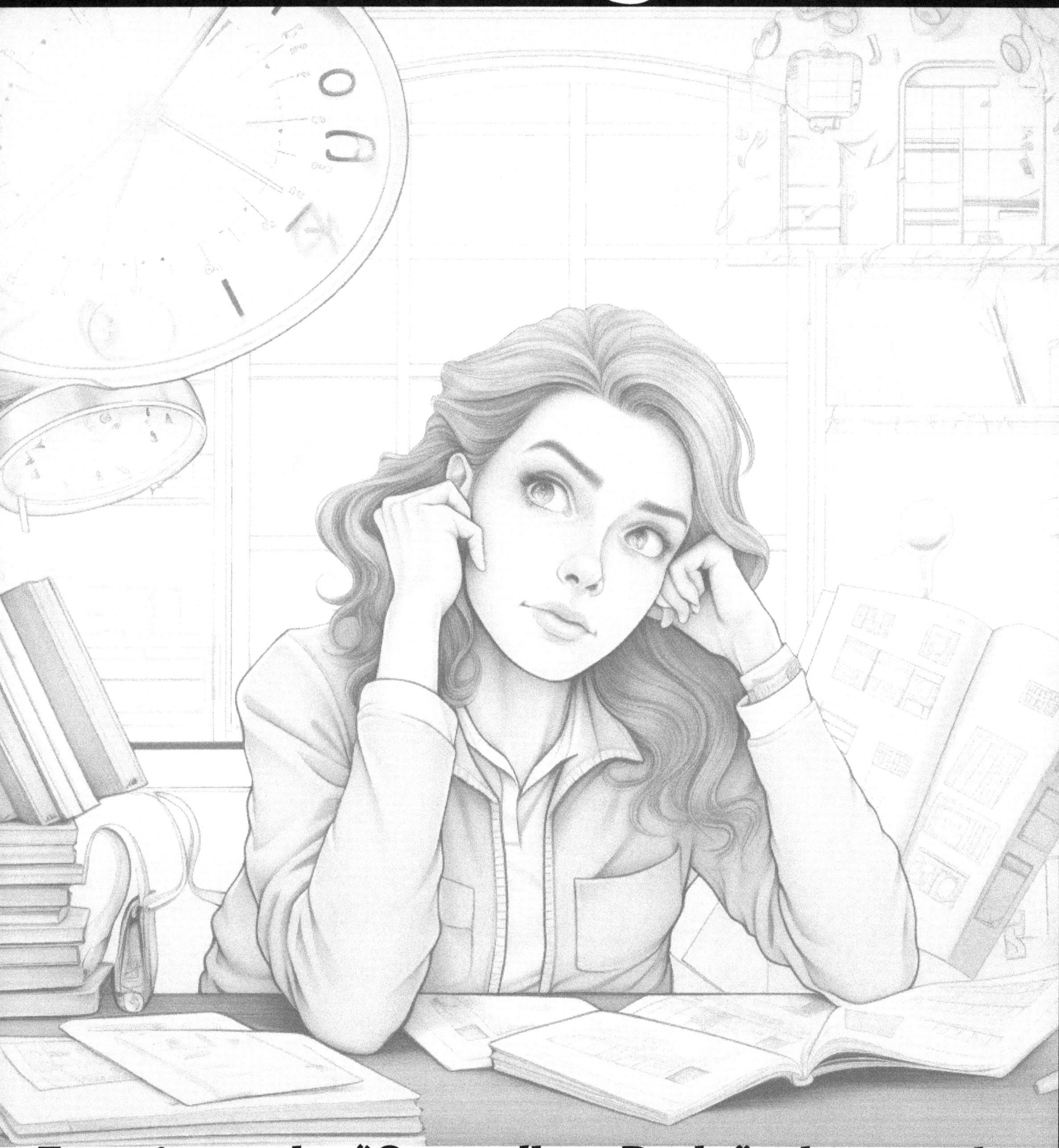

Experience the "Groundhog Desk," where each day feels like the one before, trapped in an endless loop.

Train to Nowhere

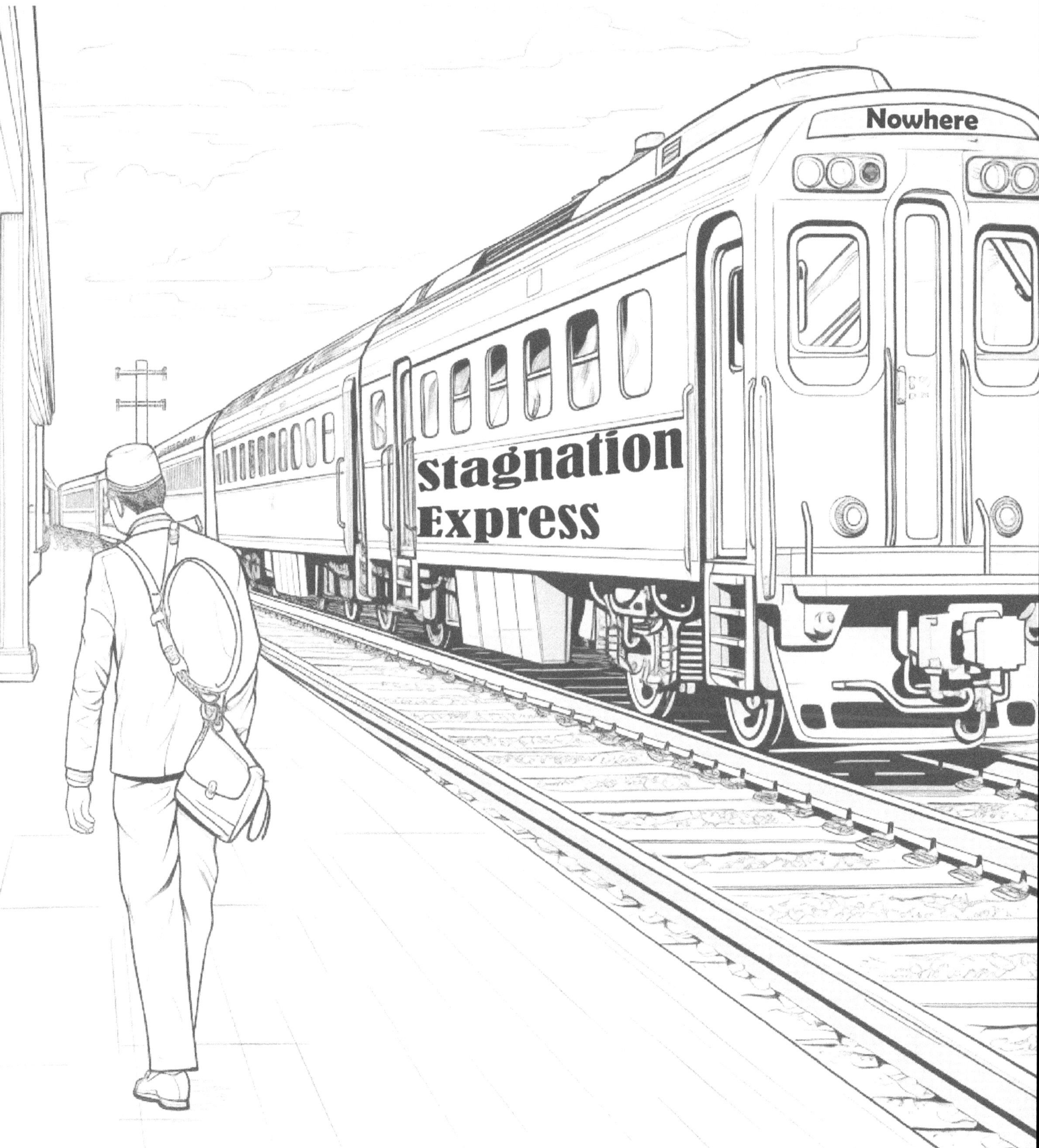

All aboard the Stagnation Express, where the train of progress only departs to stay parked on the tracks of monotony.

Mysteries of Mediocrity

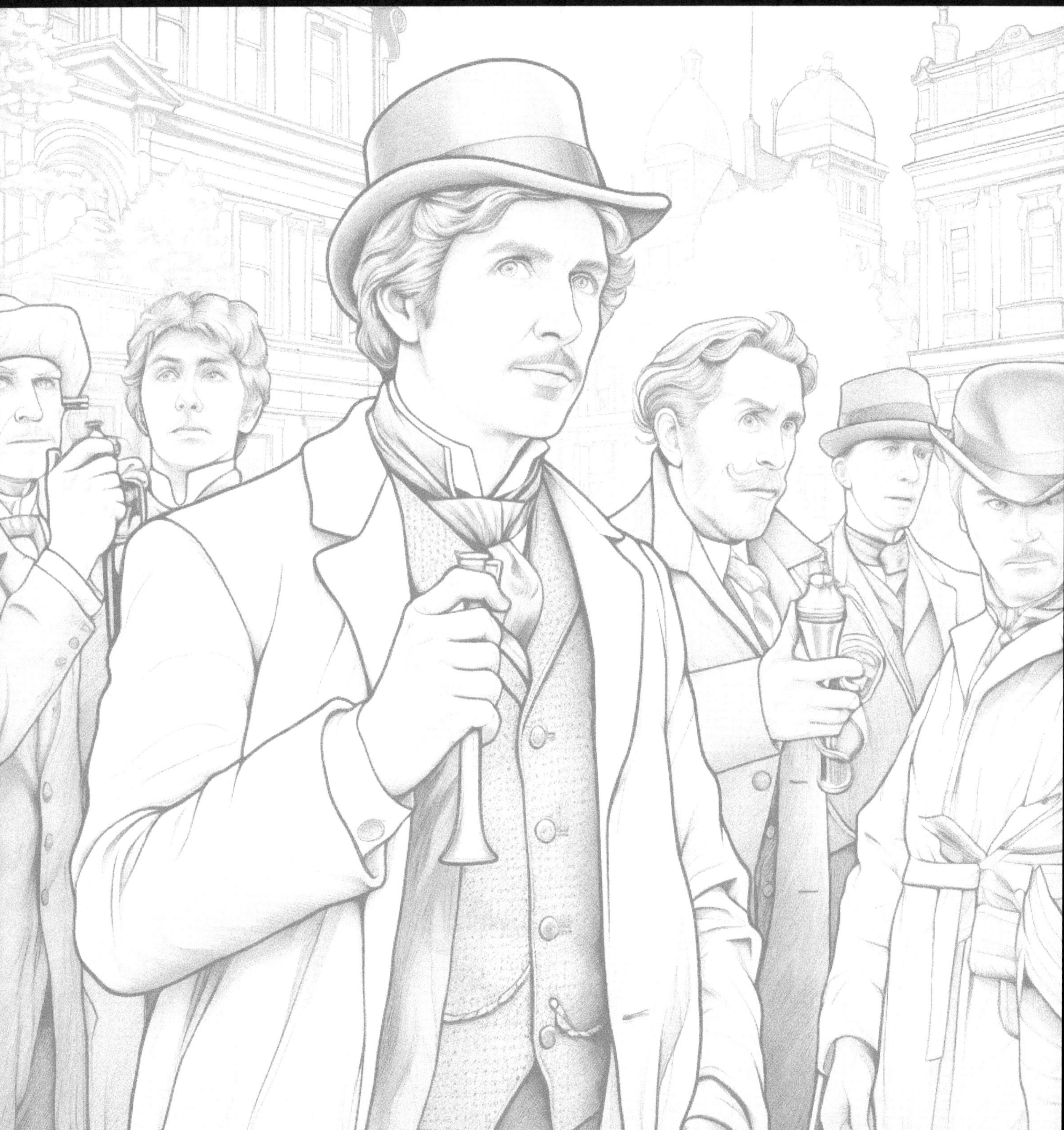

Join forces with your boss to uncover the Mysteries of Mediocrity. Together, explore clues to solve the puzzle of fading enthusiasm.

Desk Fan Fiasco

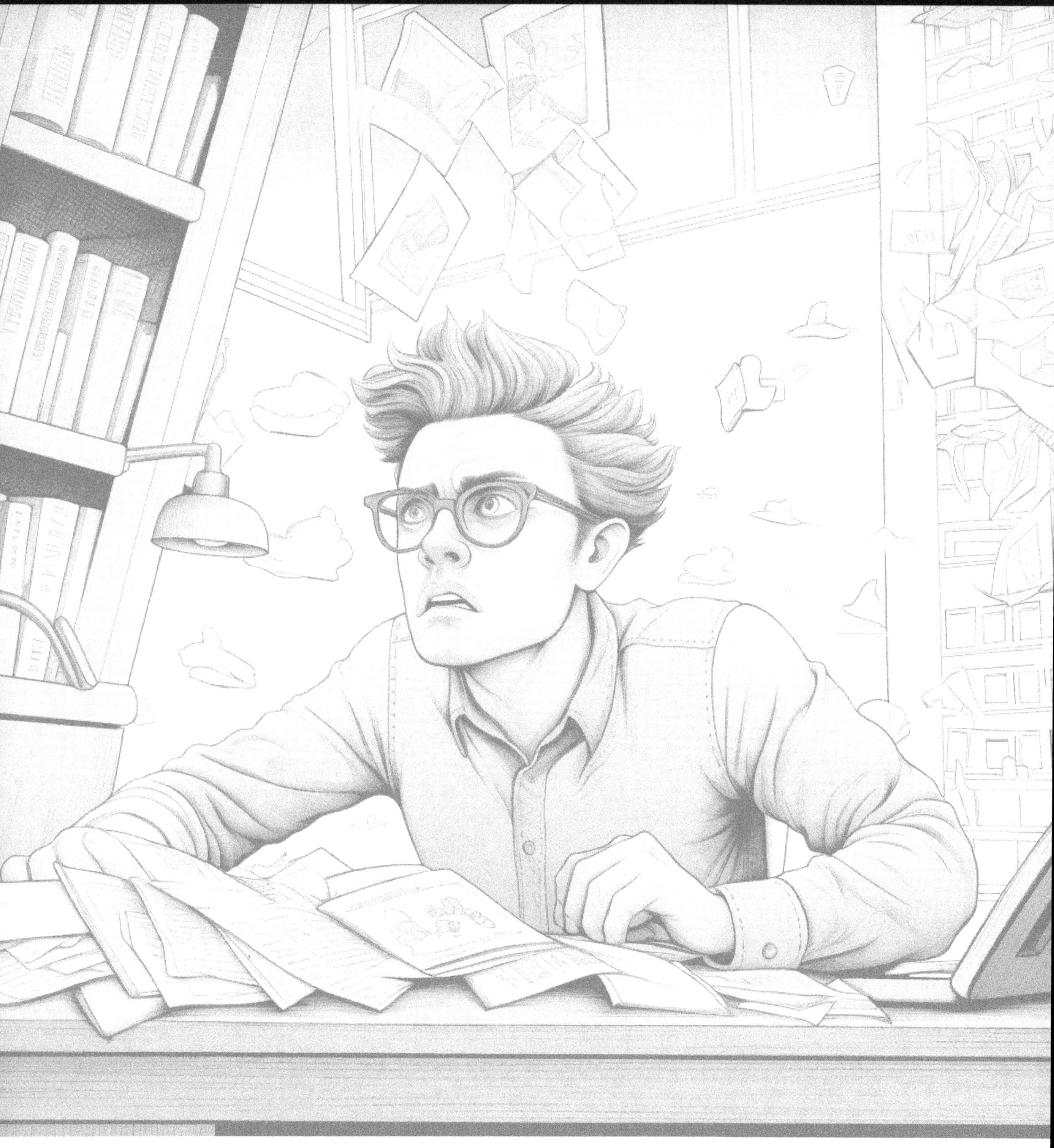

Experience the chaos of the "Papers in Flight" symphony, where fan and papers dance to their own tune.

Office Plant Drama

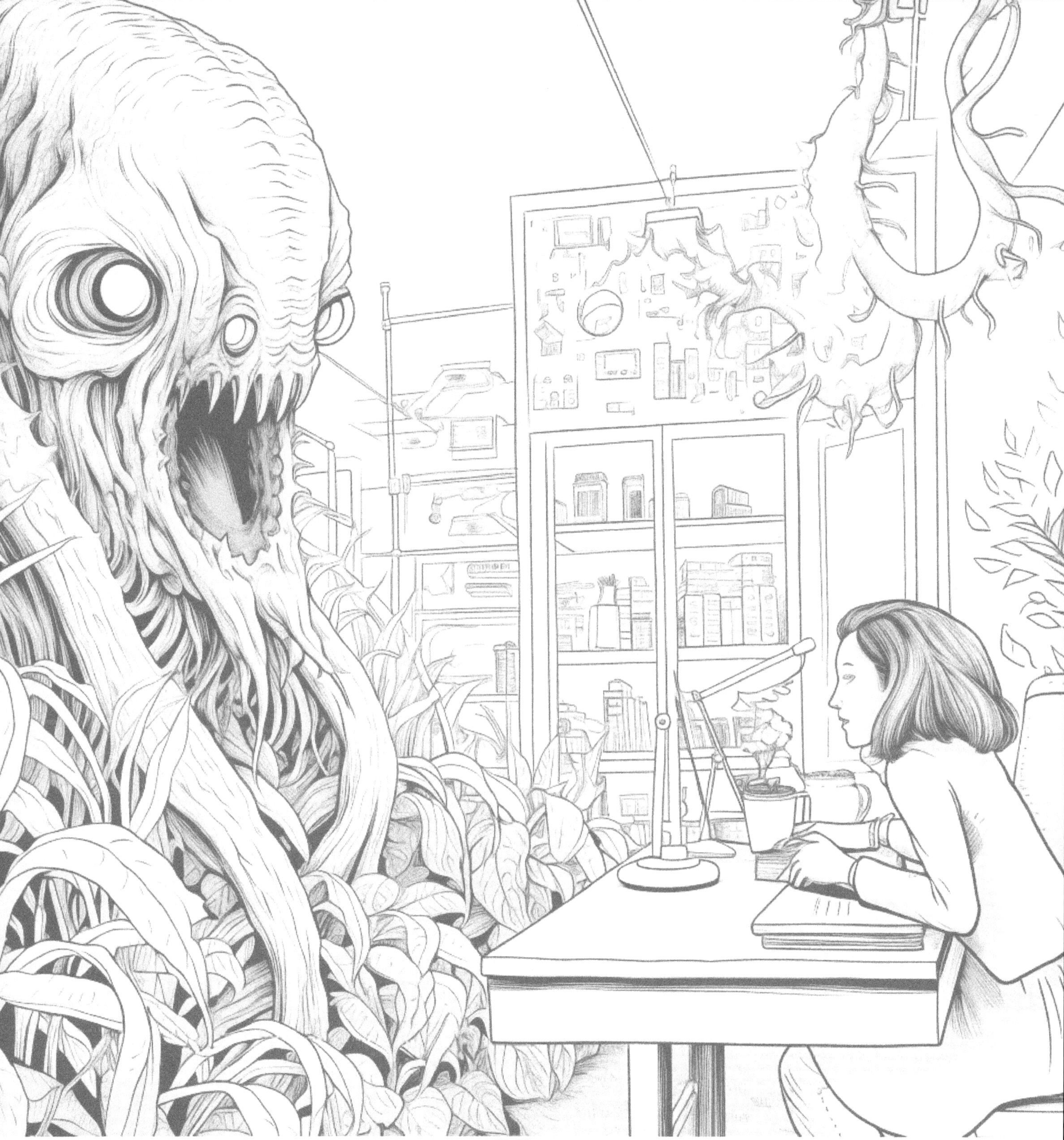

Nurturing your office plants with all the dedication of a reality TV star.

Missing Gratitude

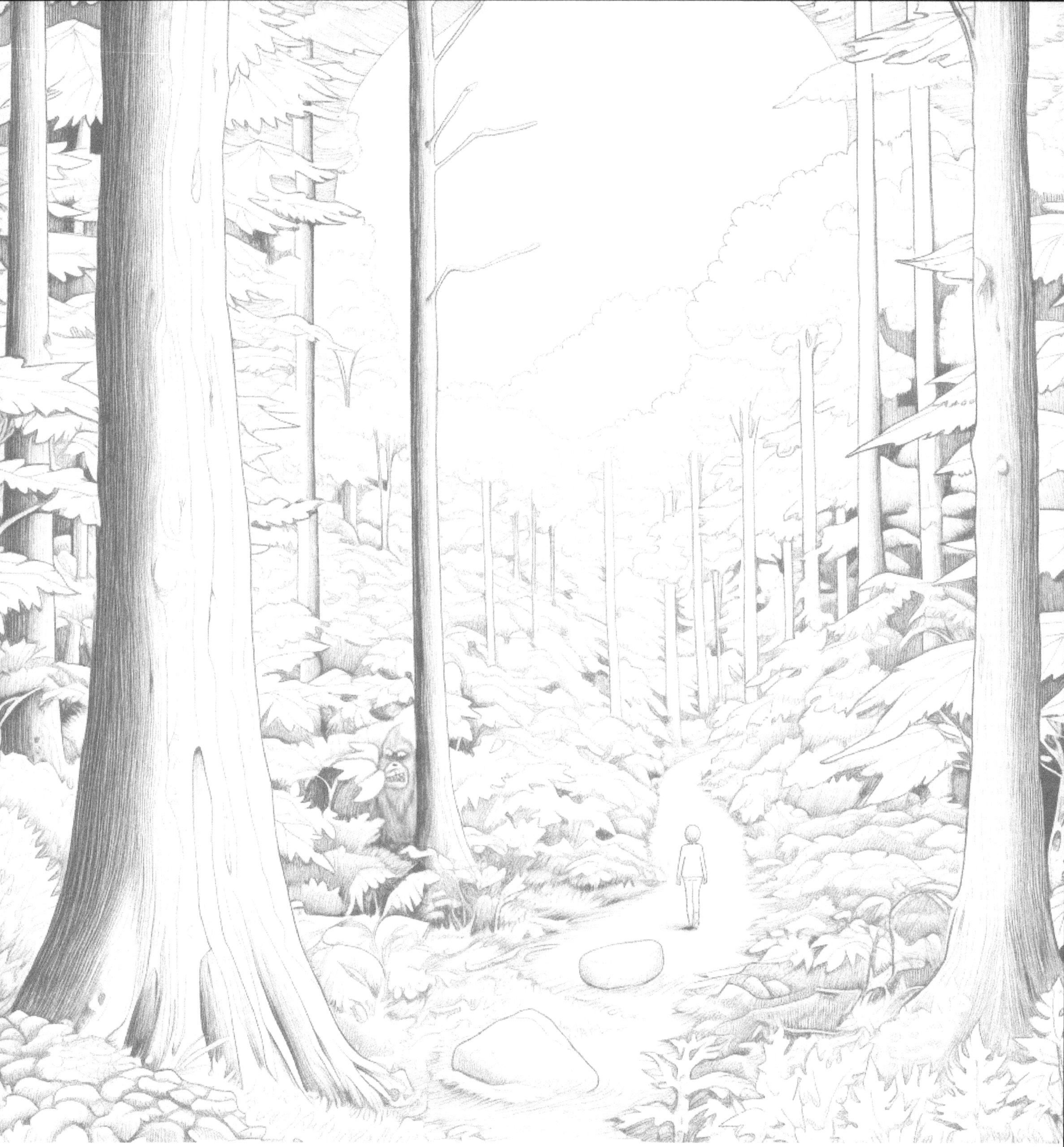

Solve the riddle of why appreciation from management feels as elusive as Bigfoot sightings.

The Oracle Desk

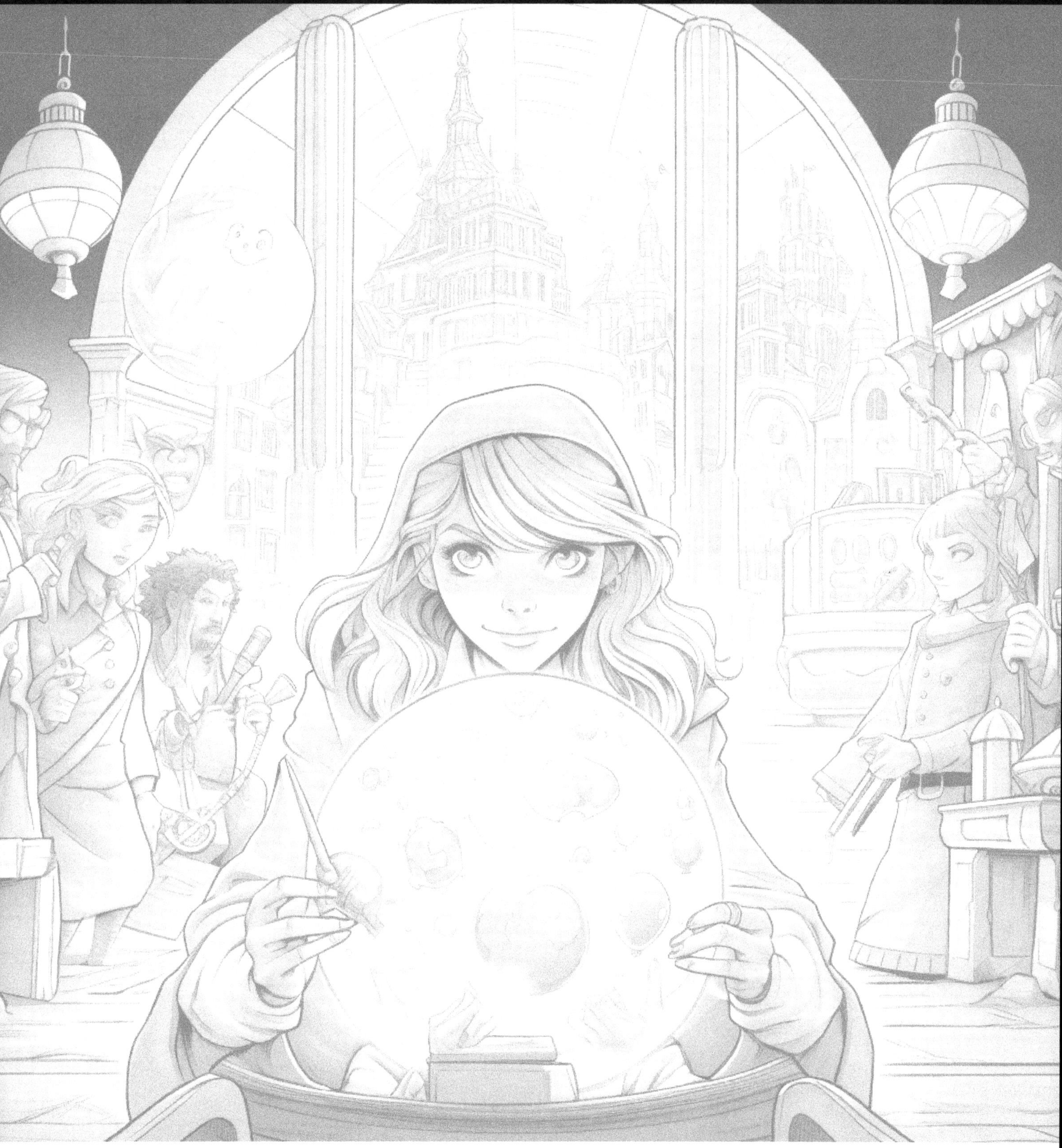

Uncover the mysteries of the "Oracle Desk," where you are the chosen one, summoned to provide answers that Google could provide in a heartbeat.

PowerPoint Purgatory

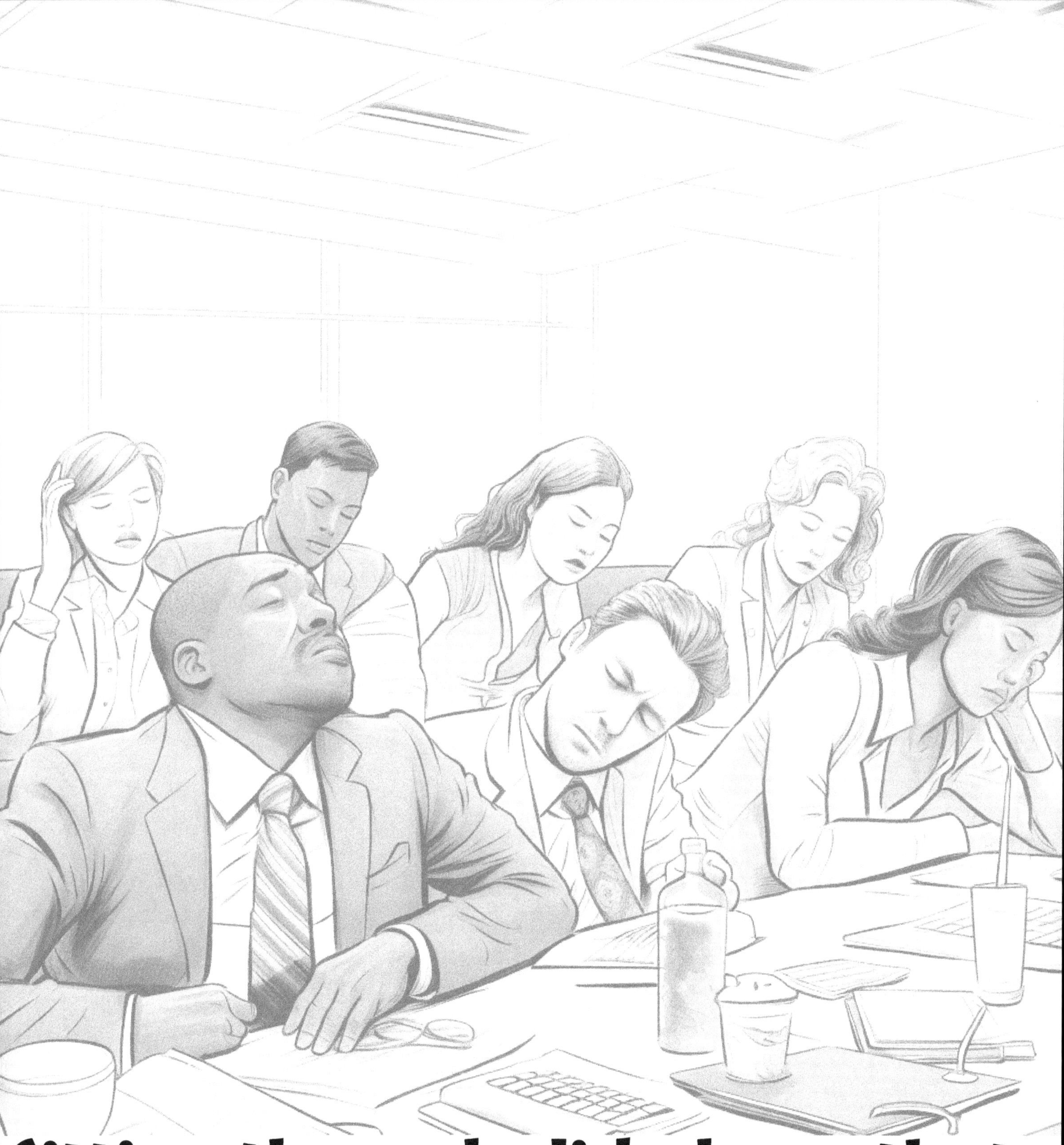

Sitting through slideshows that could cure insomnia.

Casual Friday Fantasy

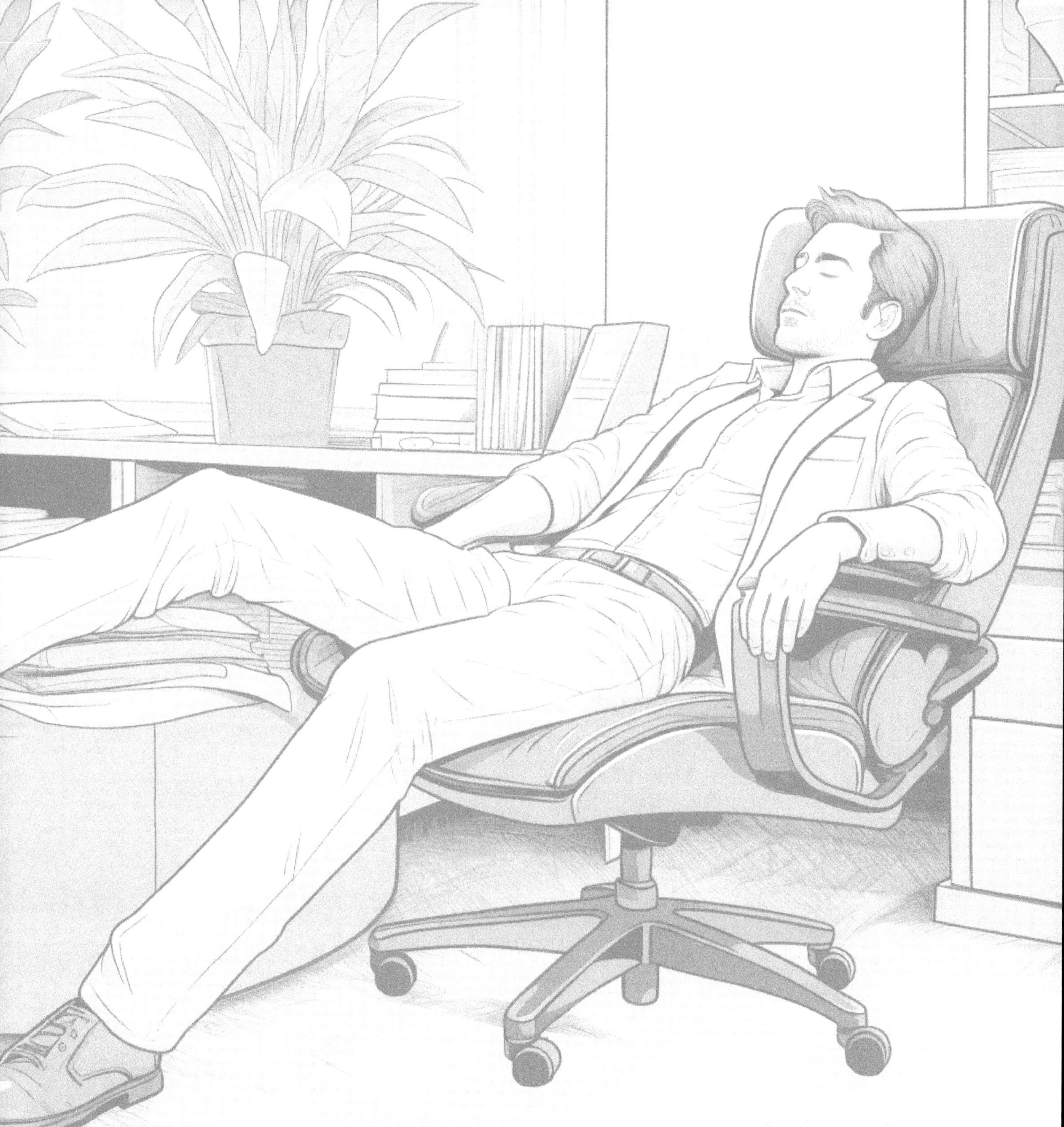

Wishing every day was Casual Friday - where "casual" means napping.

Satan's Self-Care

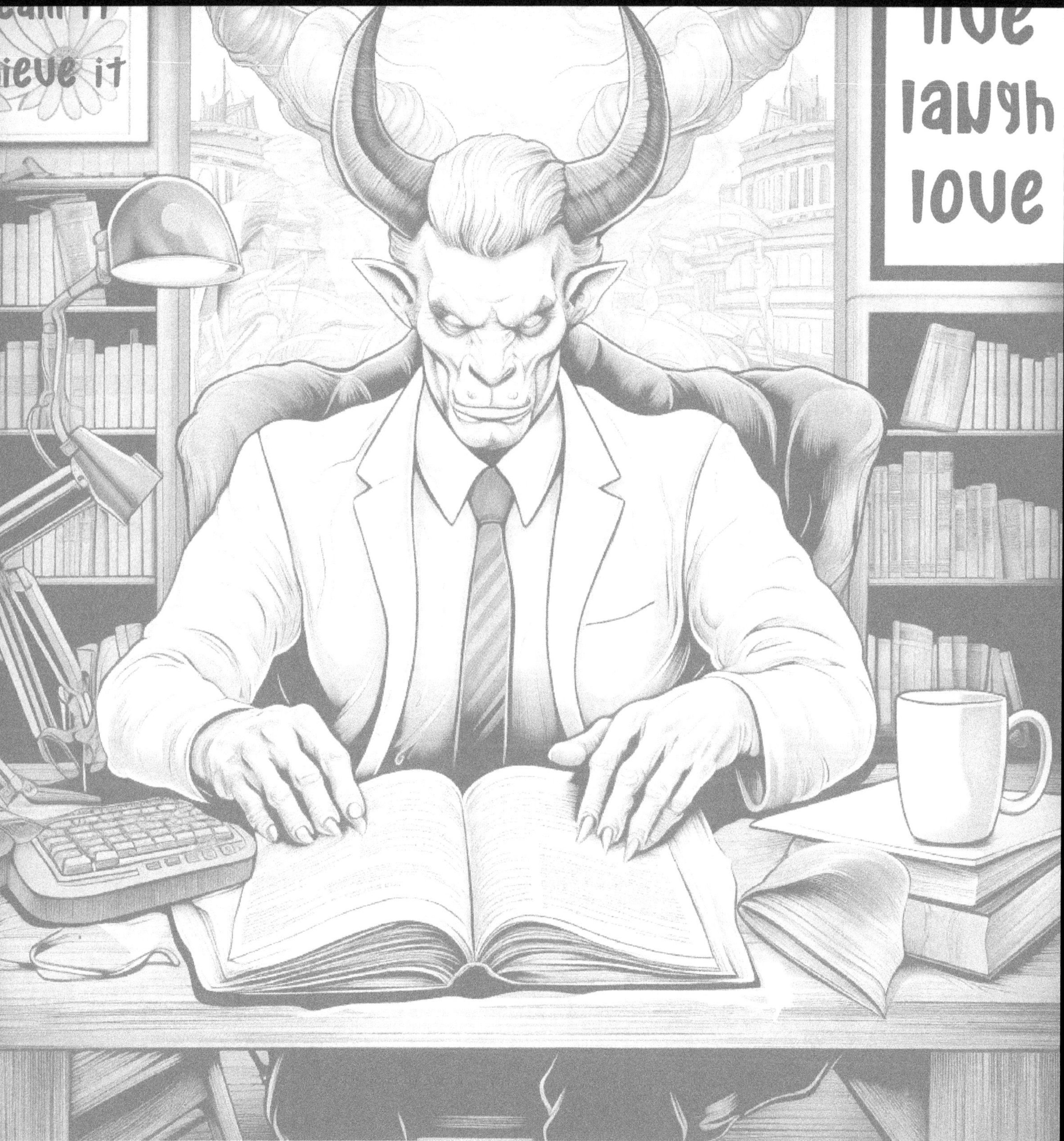

When your boss from hell tries to talk to you about self-care.

Cubicle Confusion

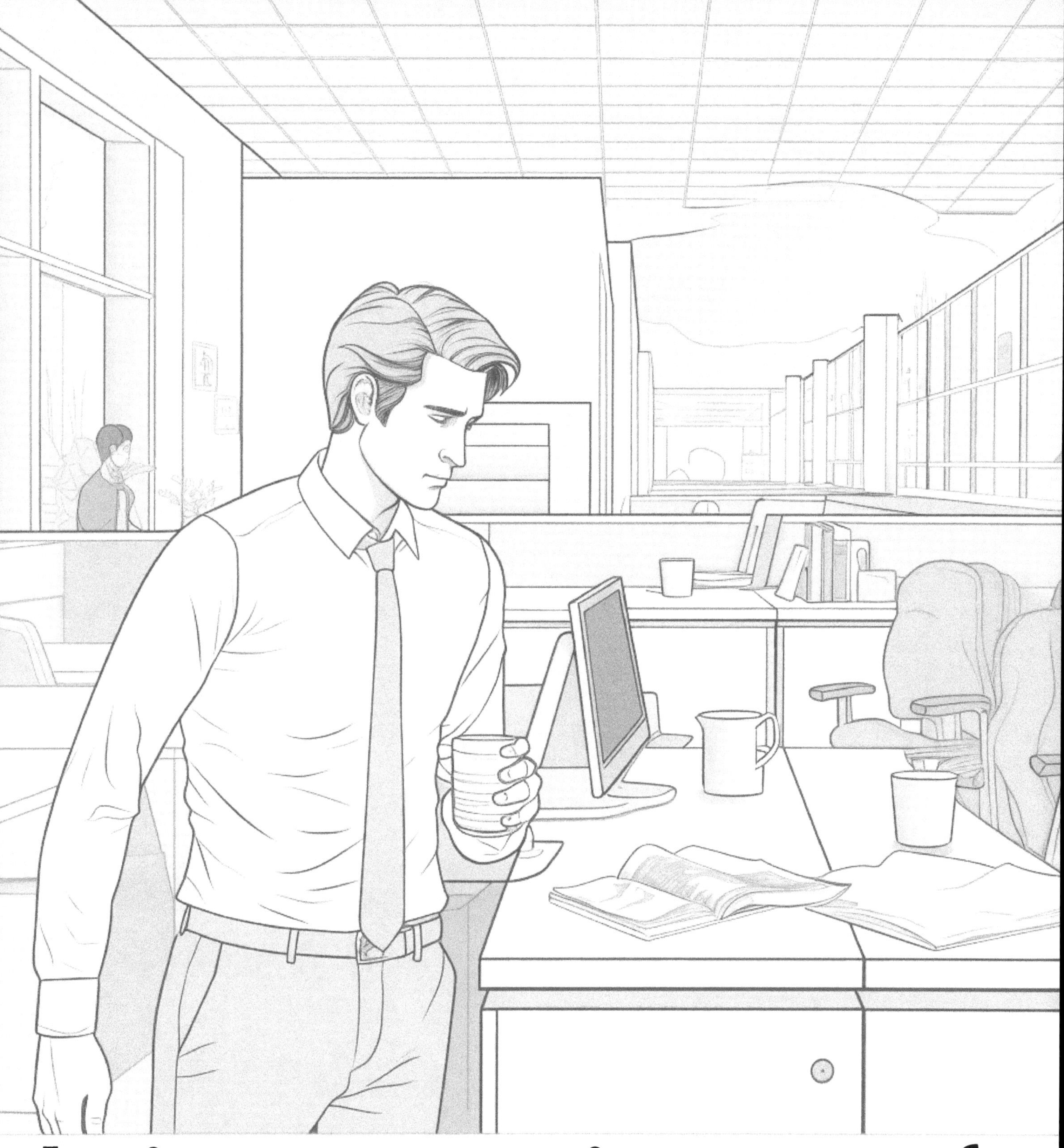

Losing your way in a maze of beige despair.

Email Avalanche

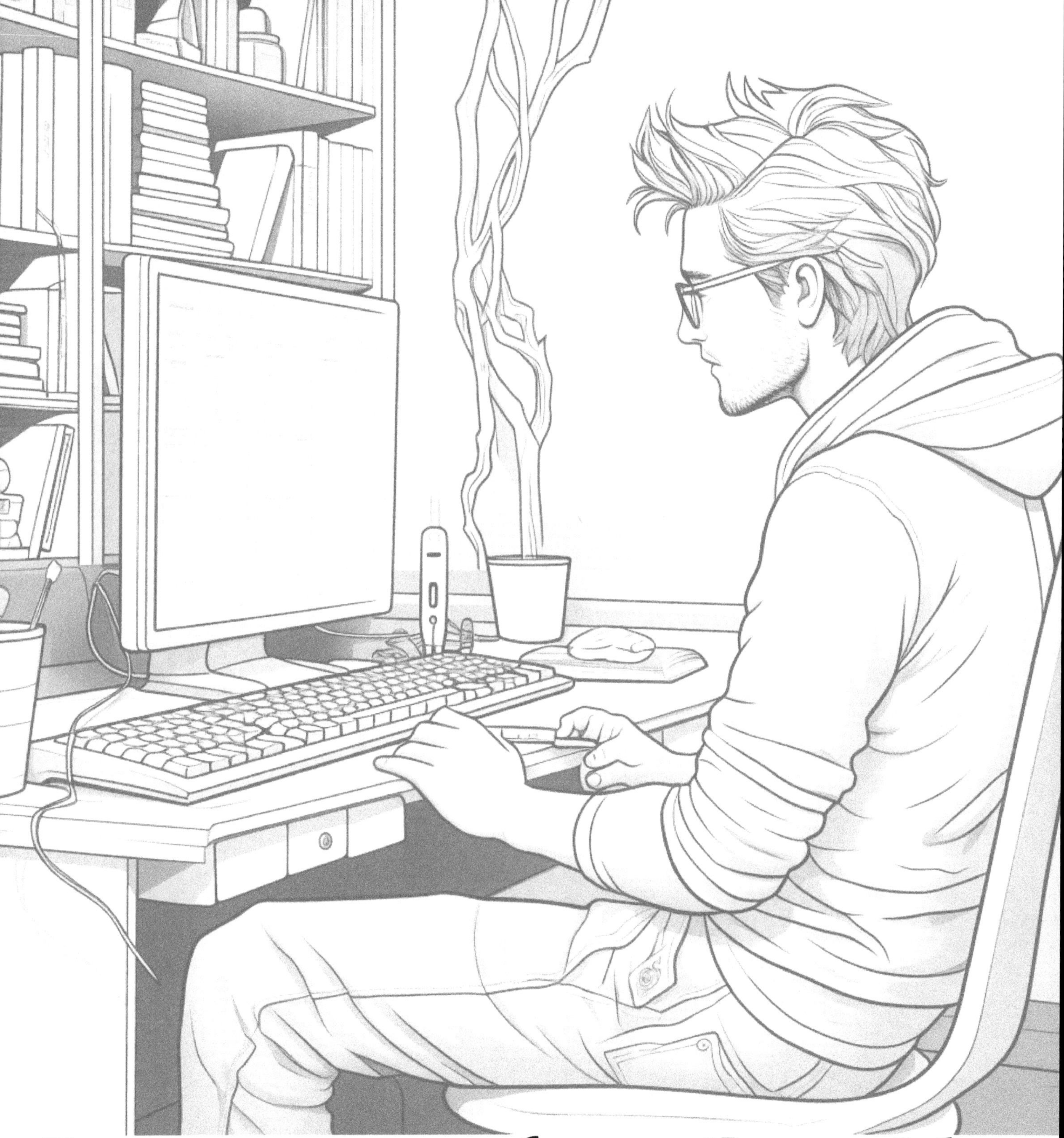

Because 99% of emails could have been a thumbs-up emoji.

Elevator Escapades

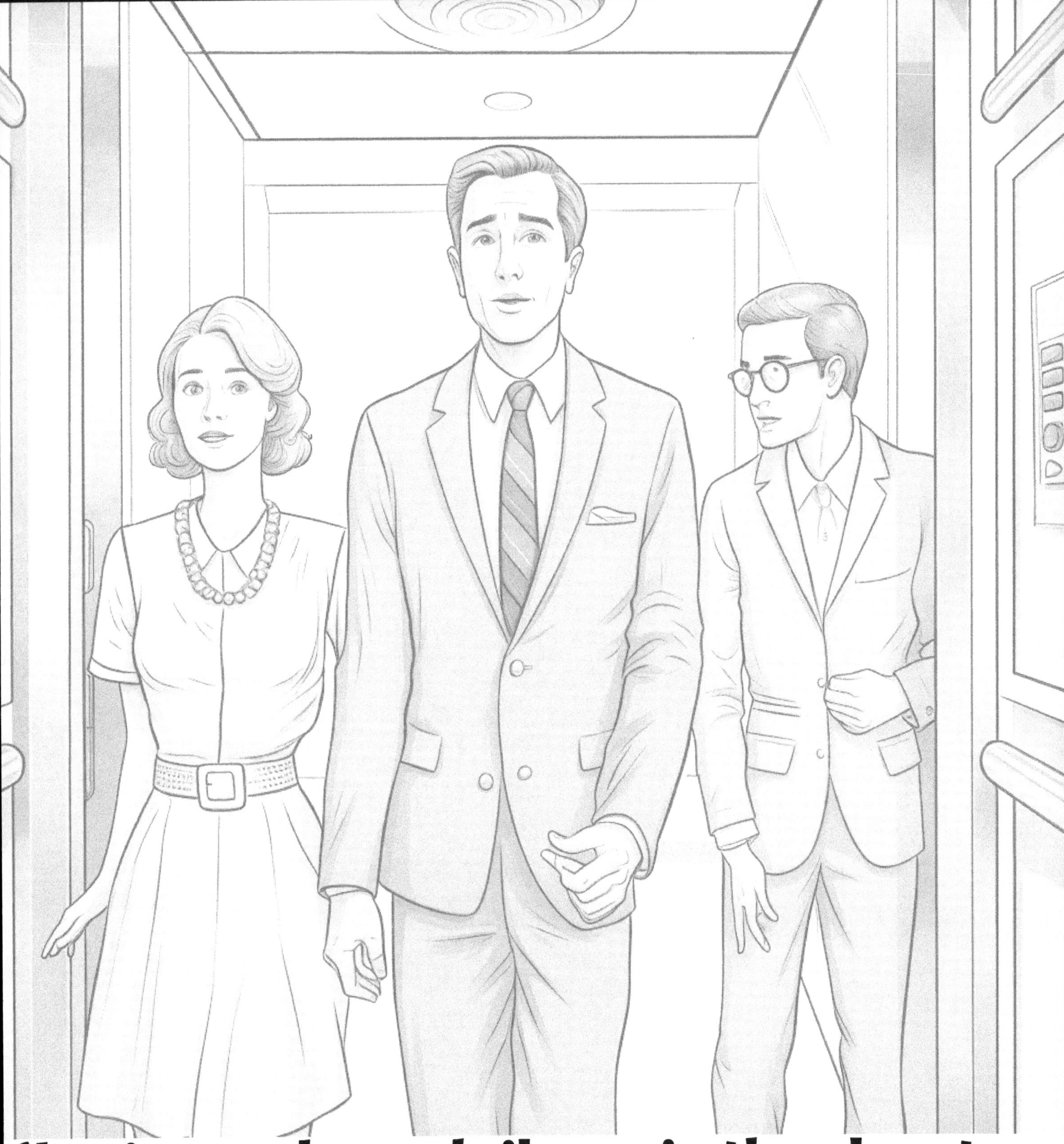

Sharing awkward silence in the elevator
- where dreams of escape thrive.

Traffic Jam Commute

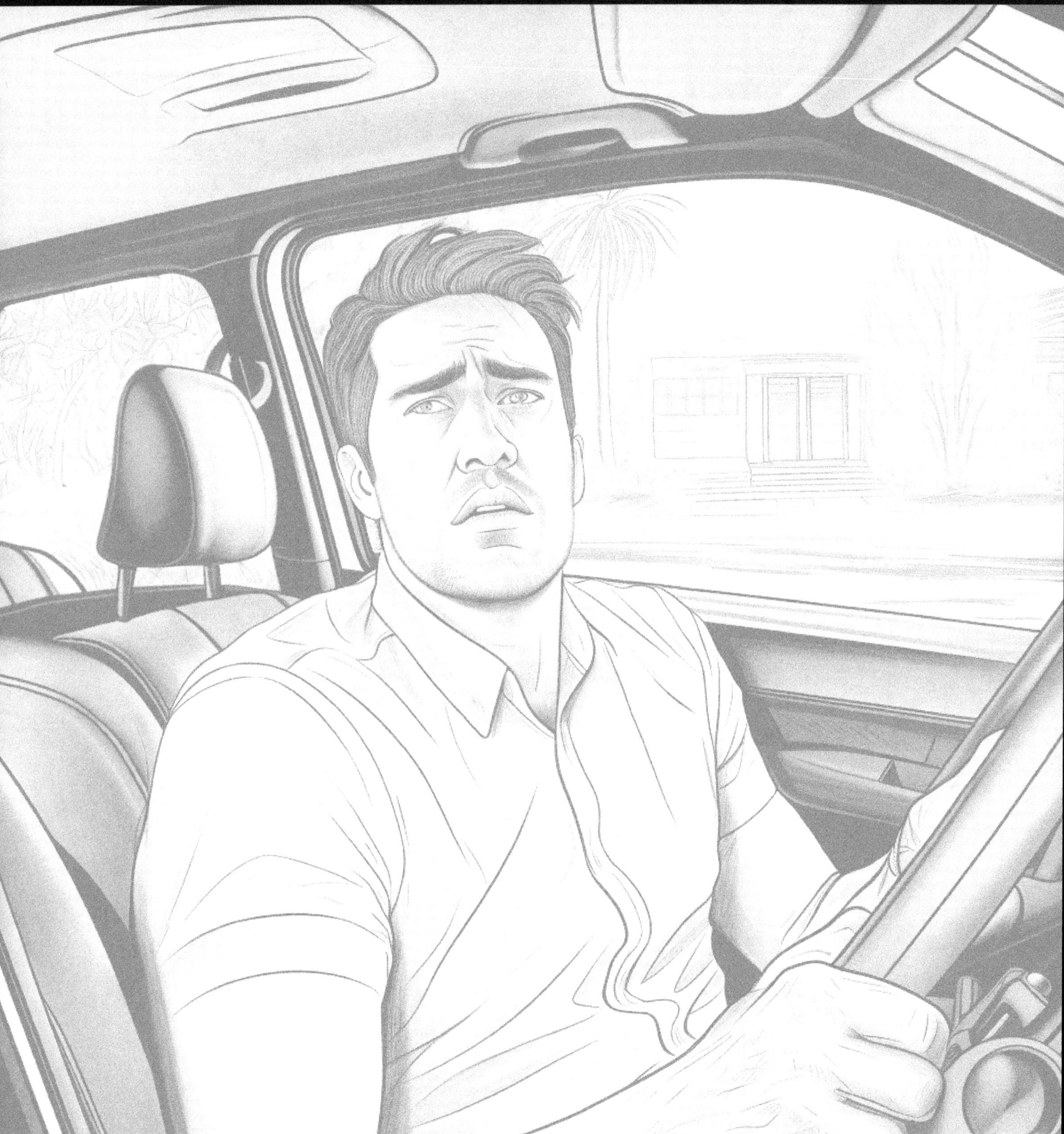

Spending more time in traffic than actual conversations at work.

Stress Ball Choreography

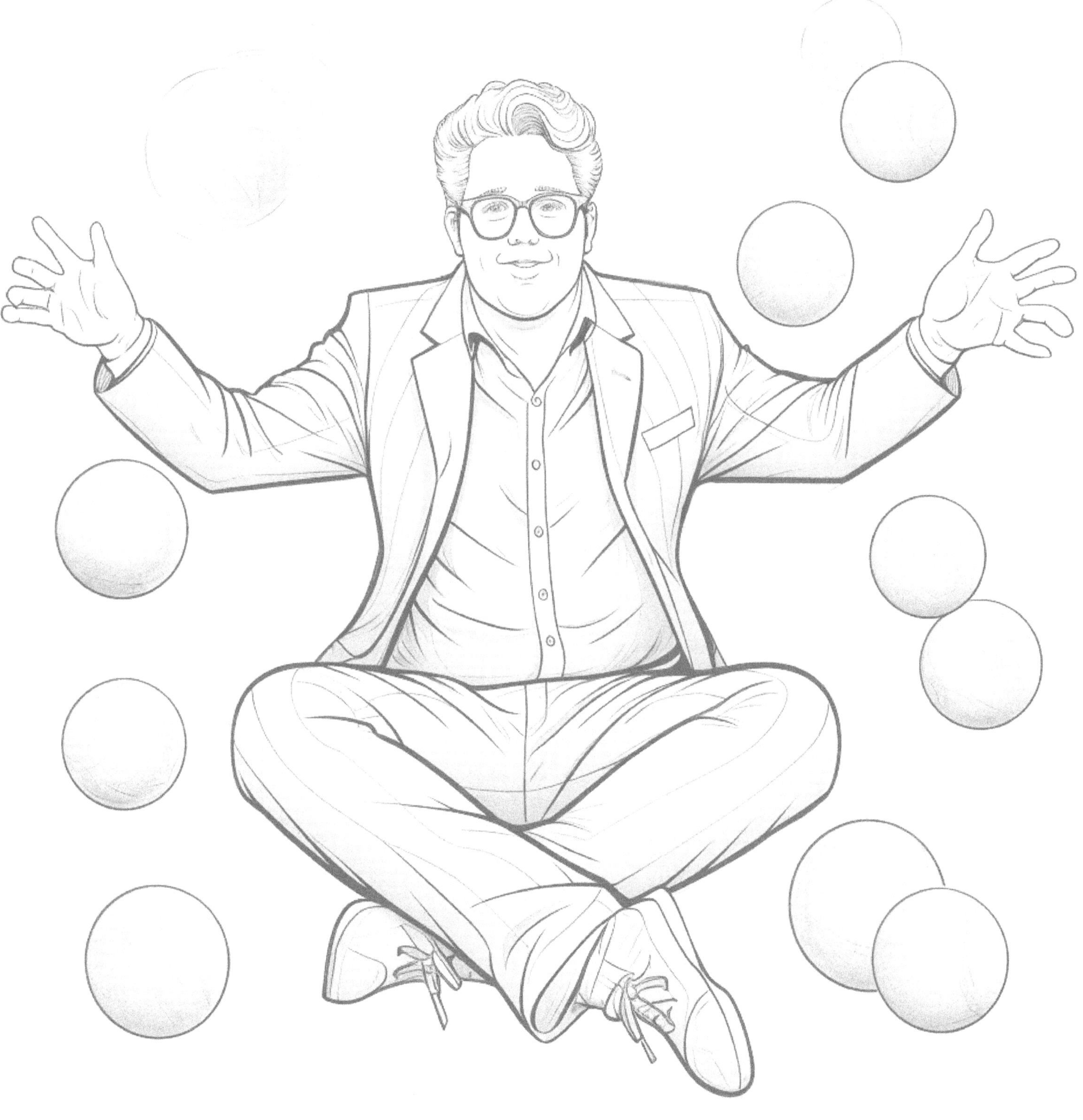

Witness the mesmerizing choreography of stress ball routines, turning anxiety into art.

Microwave Mayhem

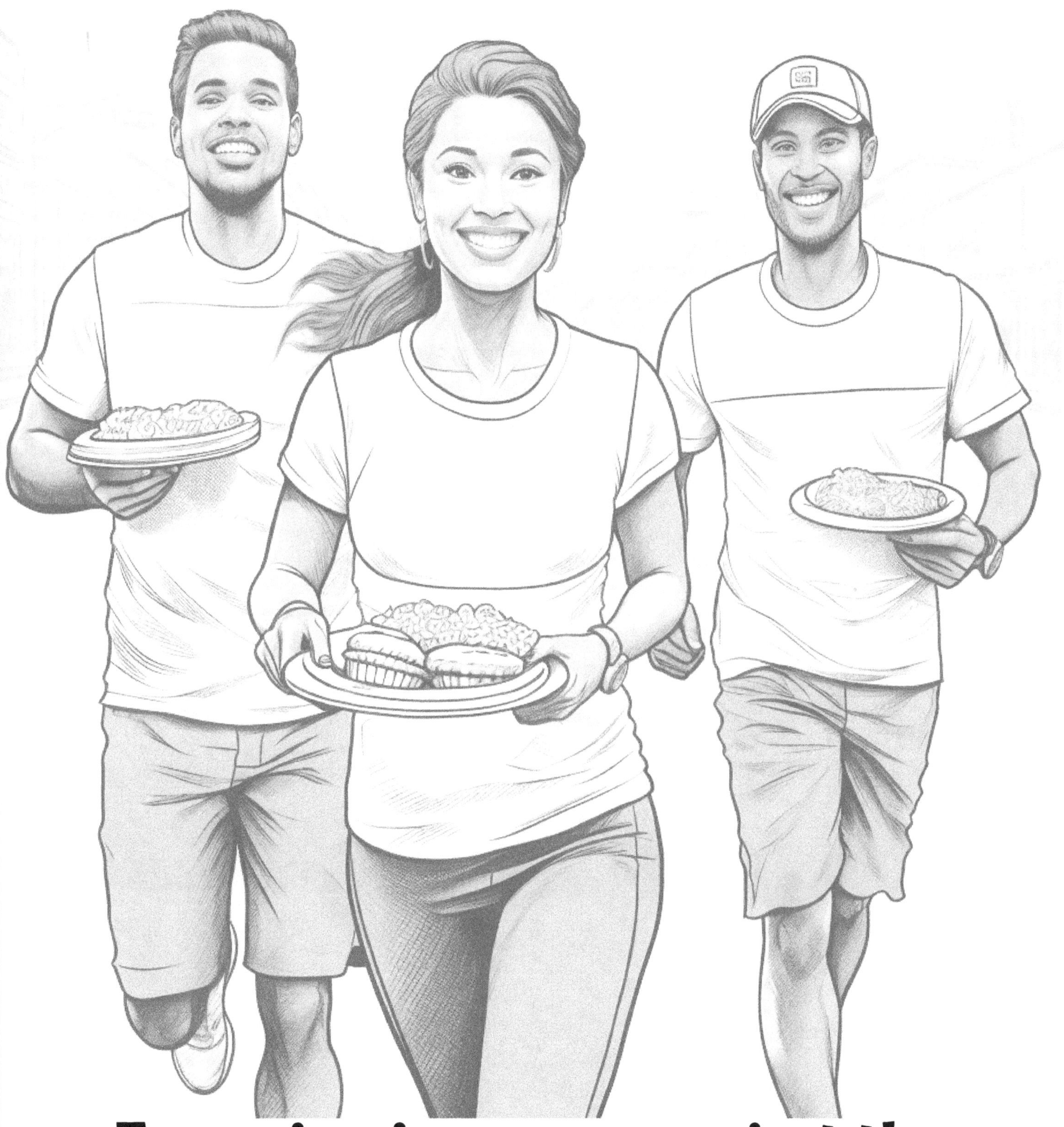

Engaging in a race against the microwave timer during lunch breaks.

Epic Snack Quest

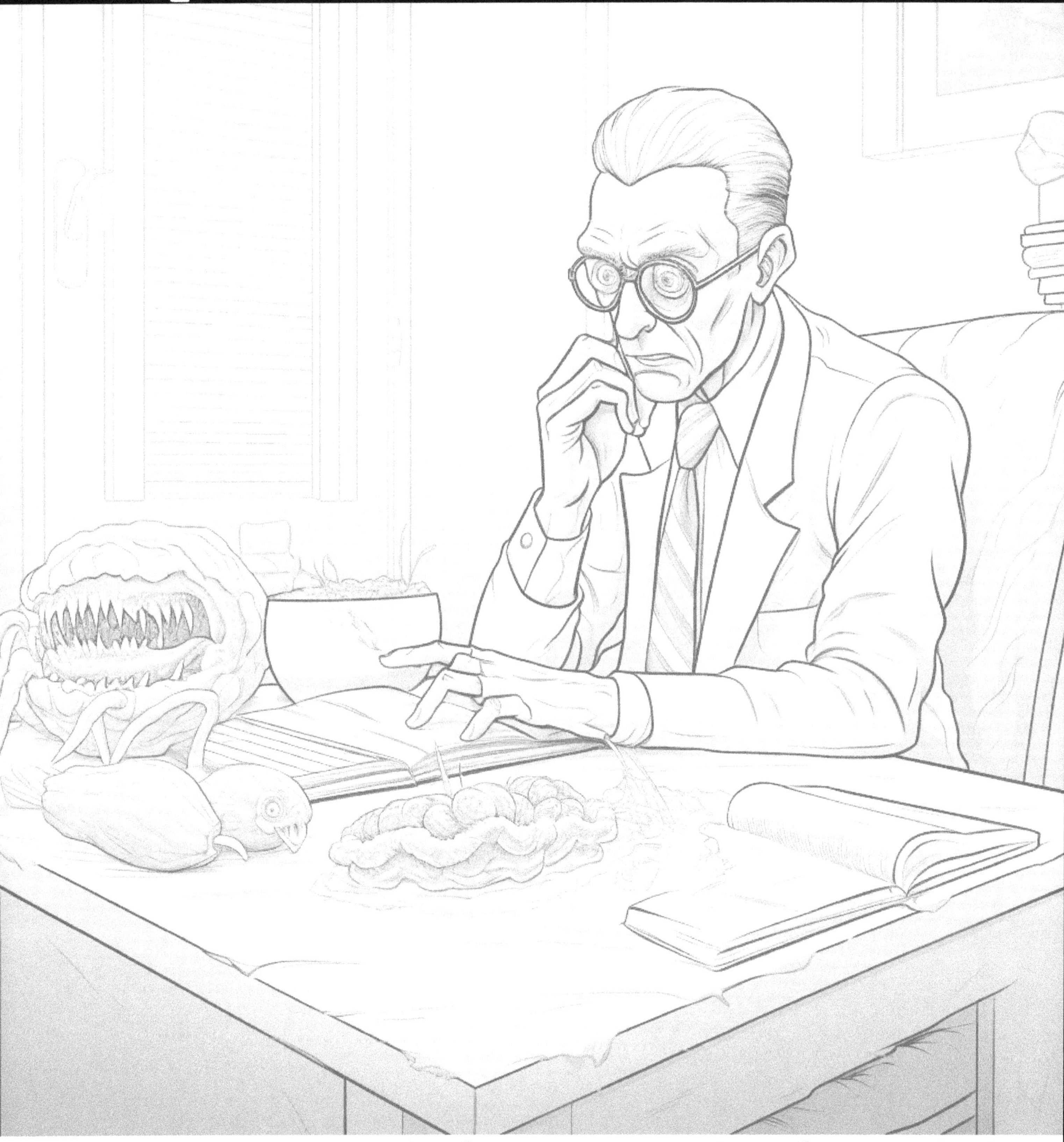

Venturing through the forgotten realm of your desk, you stumble upon an ancient monster awakened by the power of neglected snacks.

Stuck in the Loop

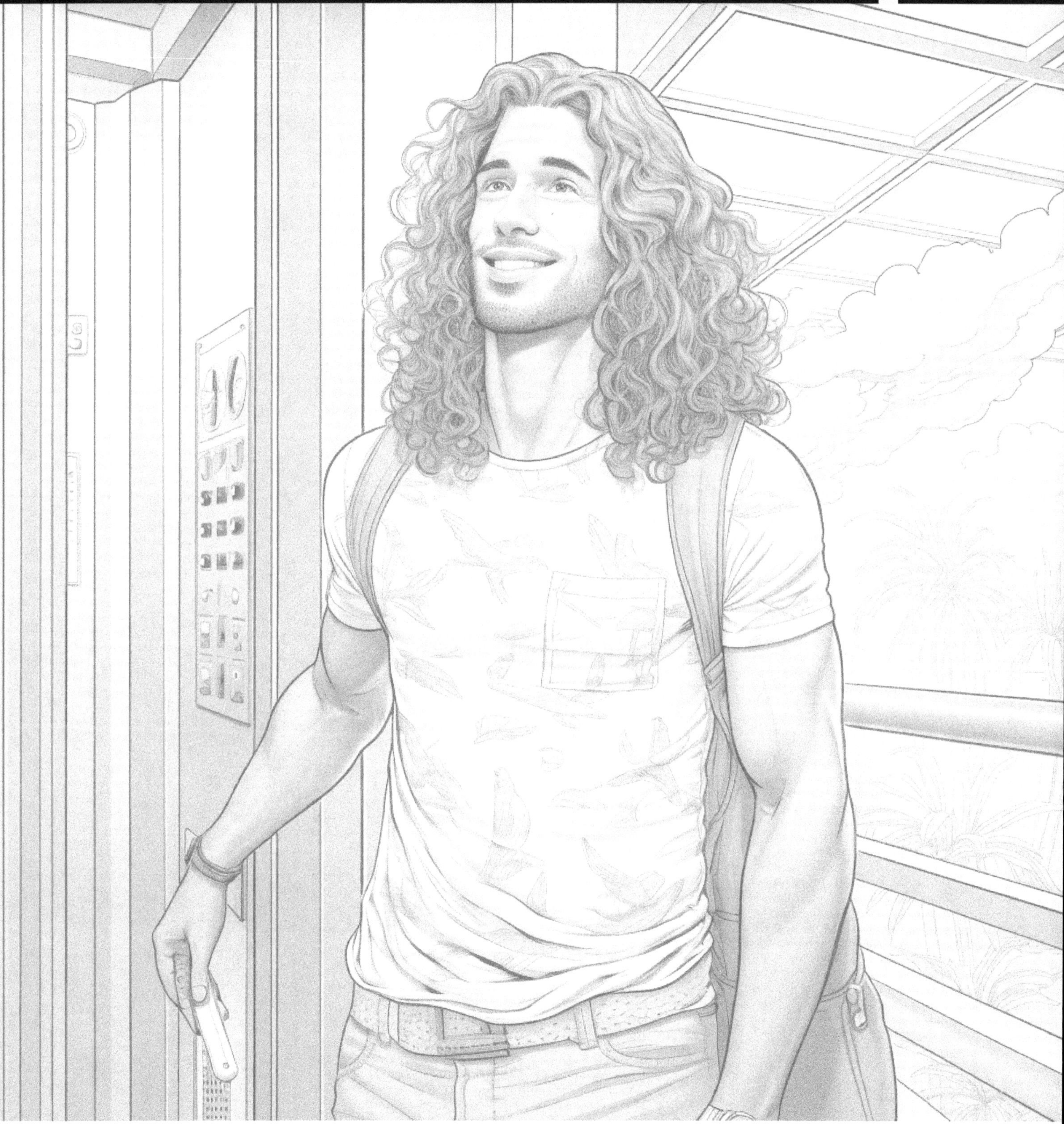

Debating the meaning of life while waiting for the elevator.

Groundhog Desk

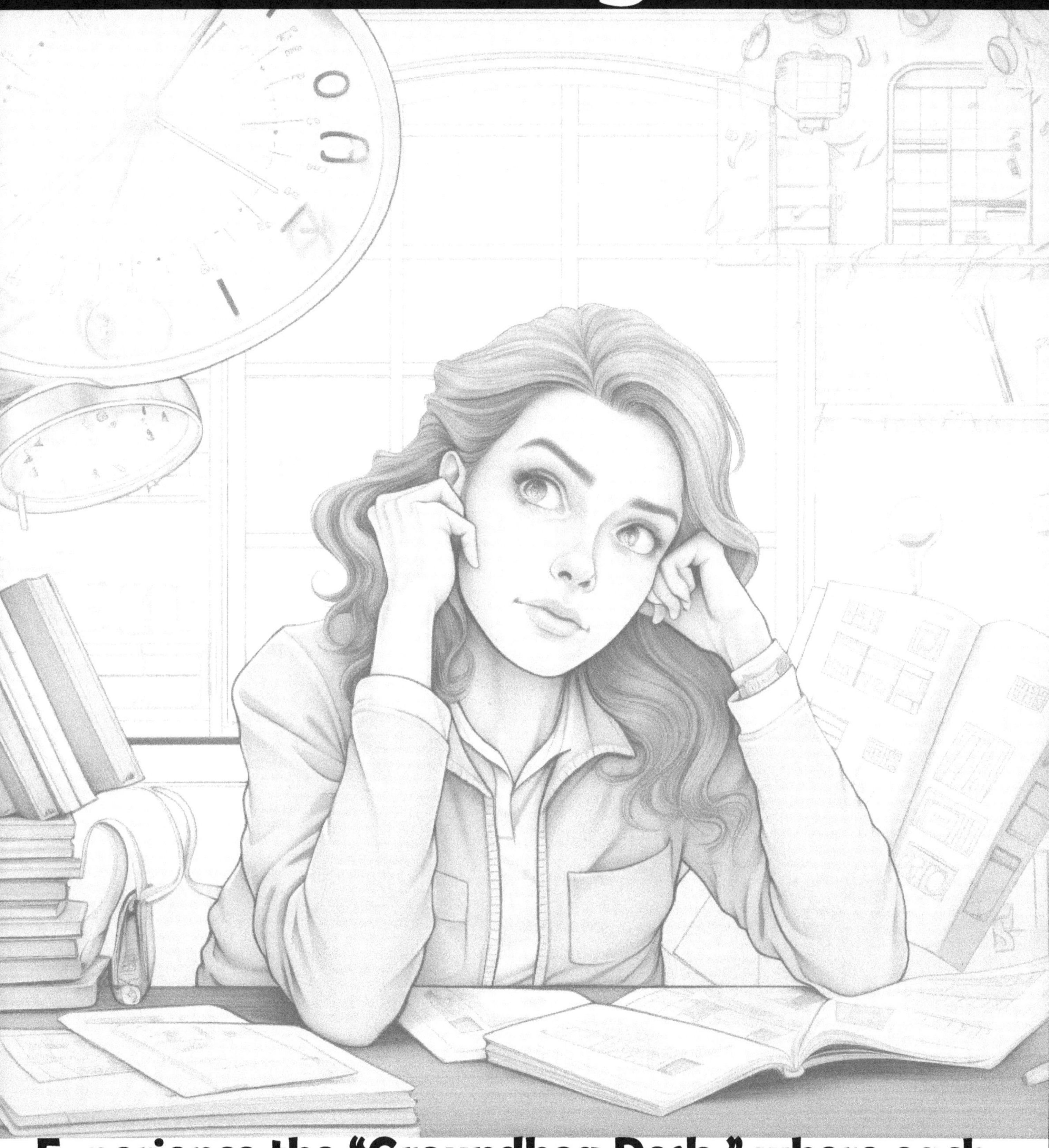

Experience the "Groundhog Desk," where each day feels like the one before, trapped in an endless loop.

Sticky Situation

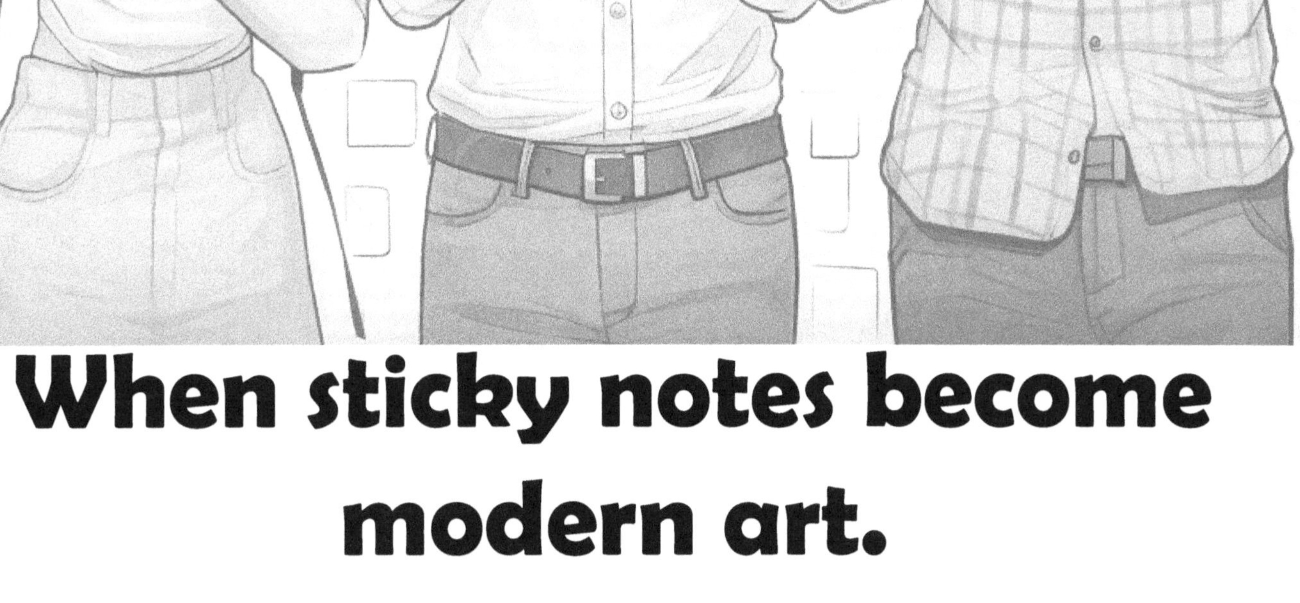

When sticky notes become modern art.

Party Pooper Problems

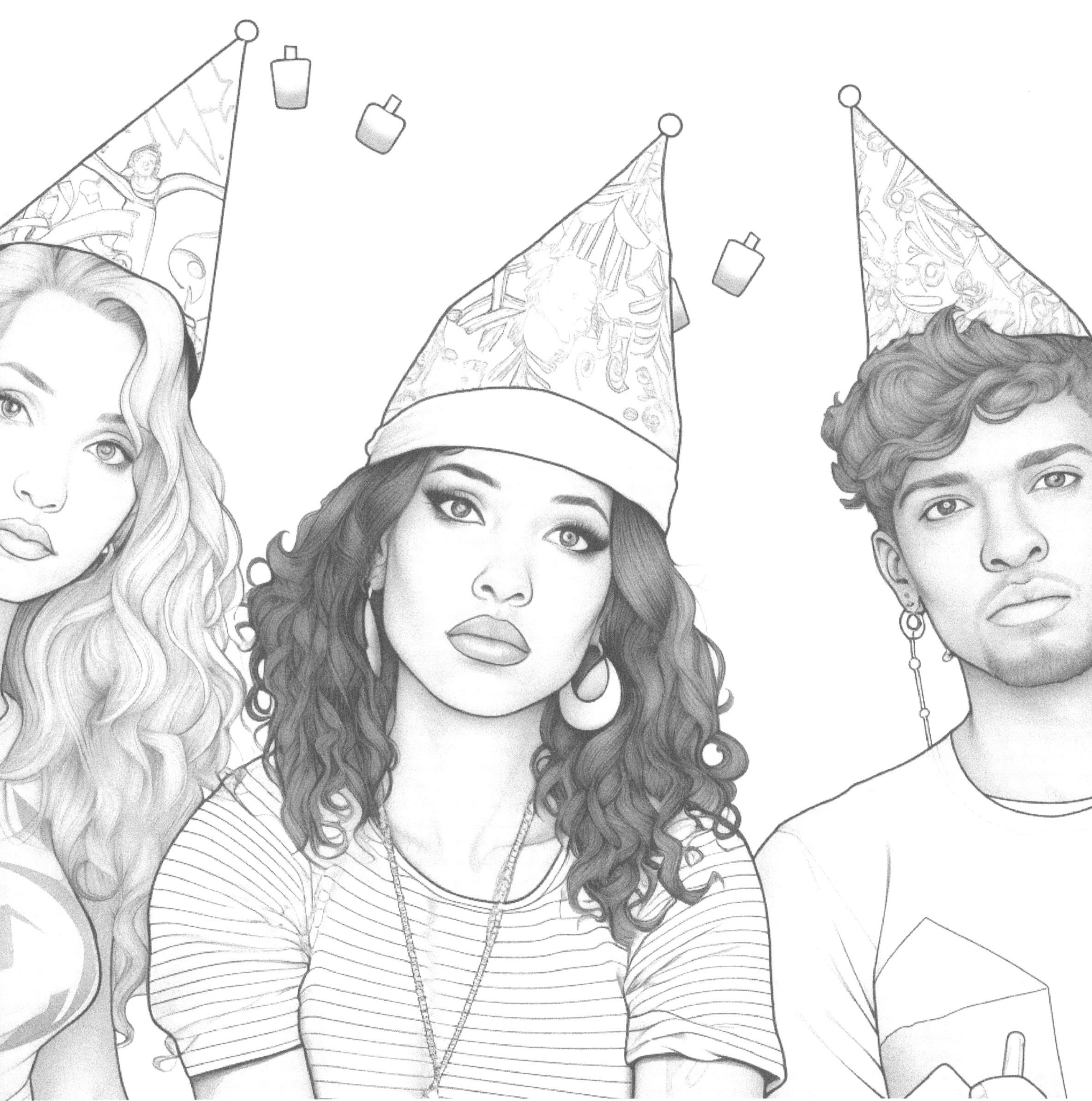

Caught in a whirlwind of regret at the mandatory company party, where small talk and awkward dance moves threaten to drown your enthusiasm.

Earplug Emergency

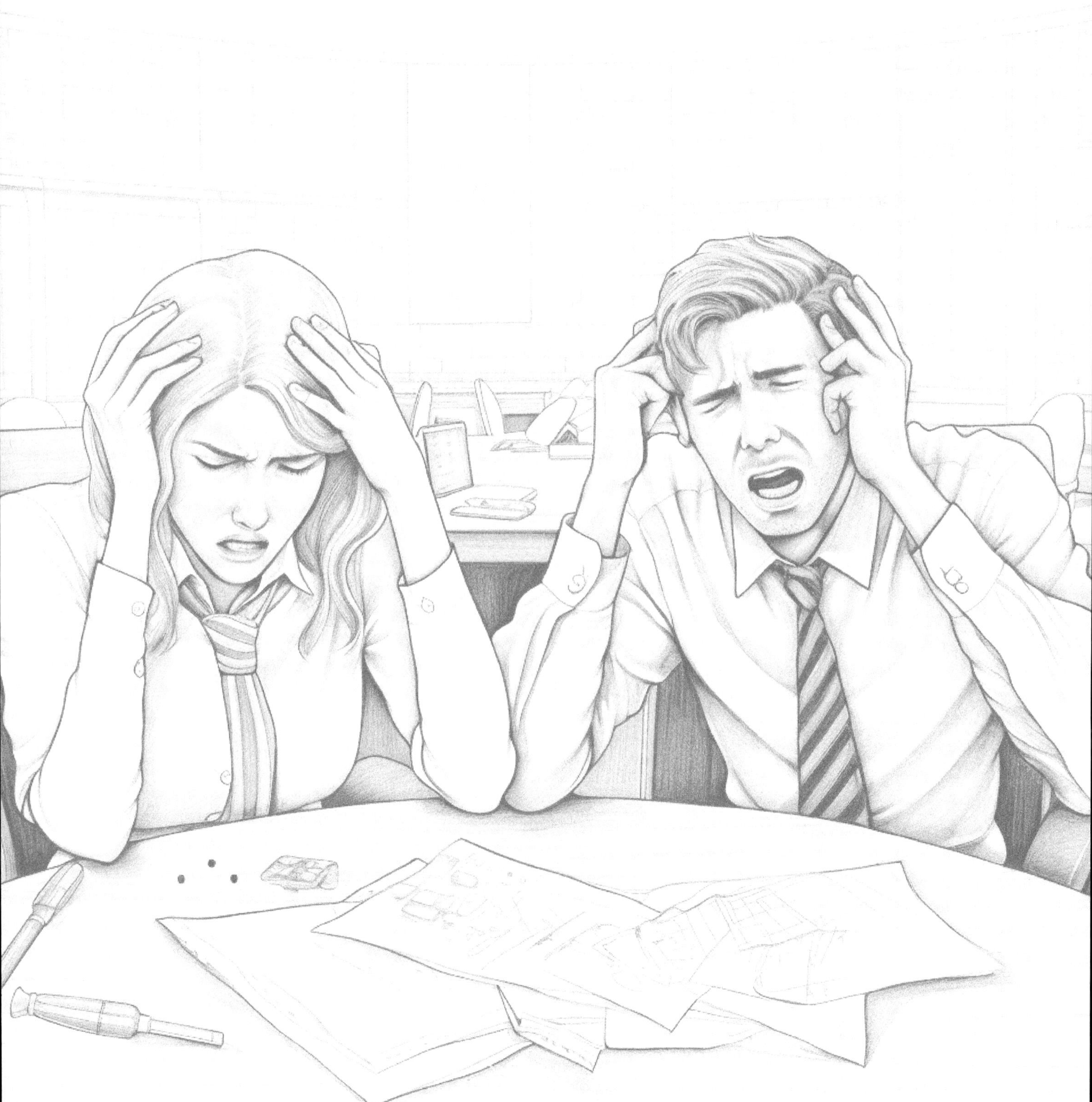

Begin the "Earplug Emergency Protocol," as you try to protect your ears from the audio assault of an enthusiastic coworker.

Swivel Chair Olympics

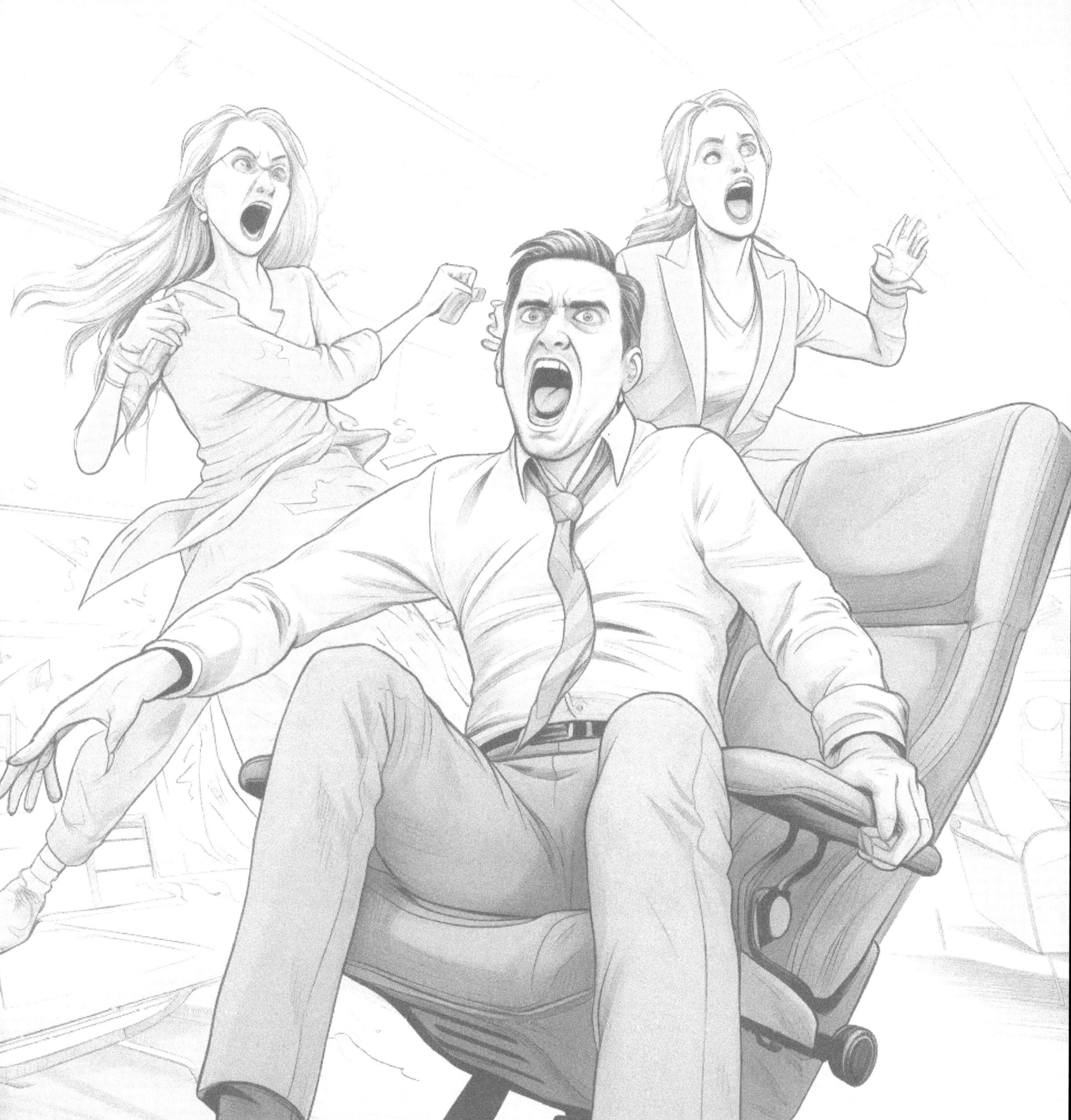

Competing in spontaneous office chair races when no one is watching.

Silent Symphony

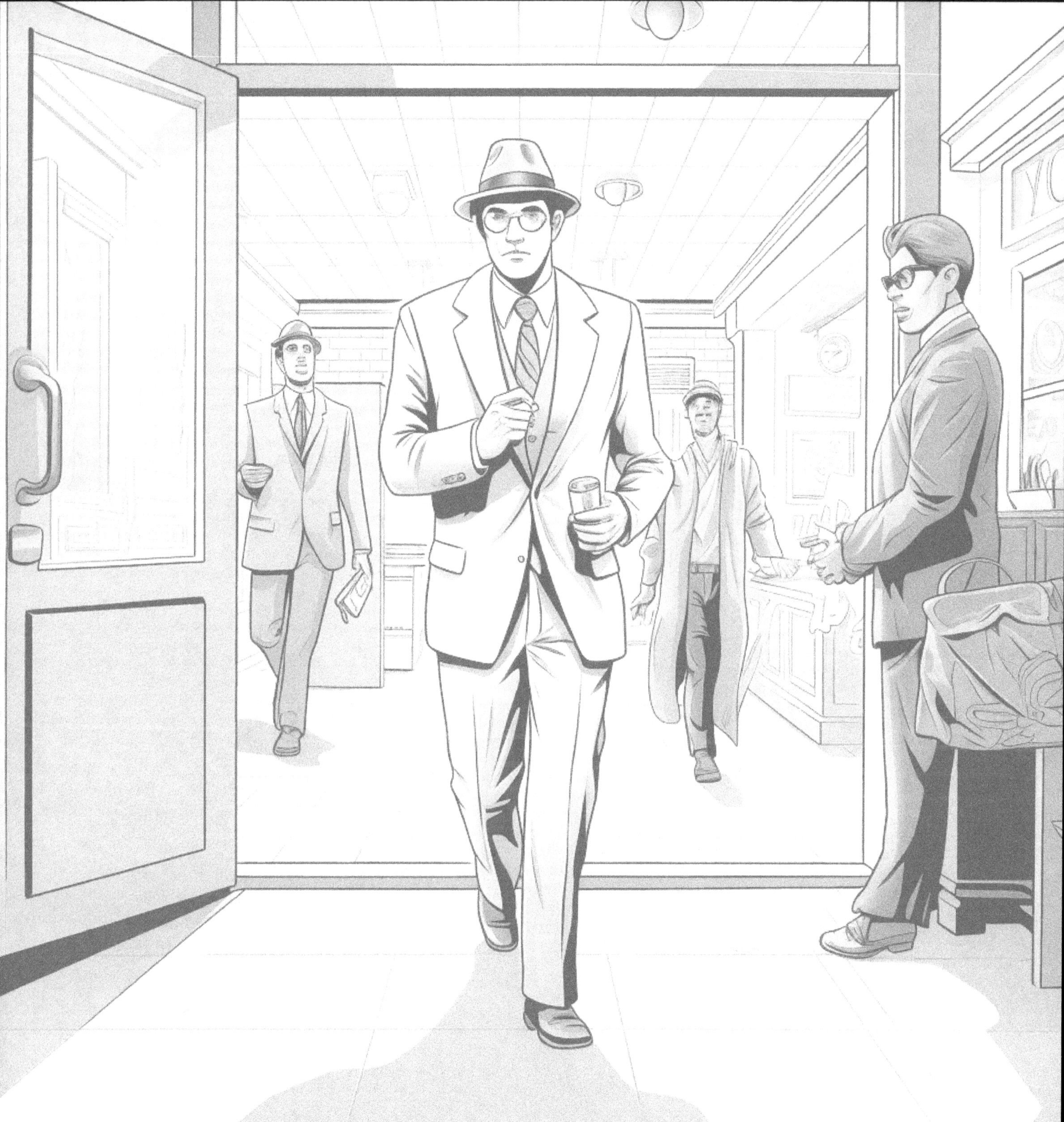

Conducting a symphony of quiet footsteps and laughter as you sneak past colleagues to reach the coveted soundproof pooping restroom.

Ctrl + Zzz: The Update Nap

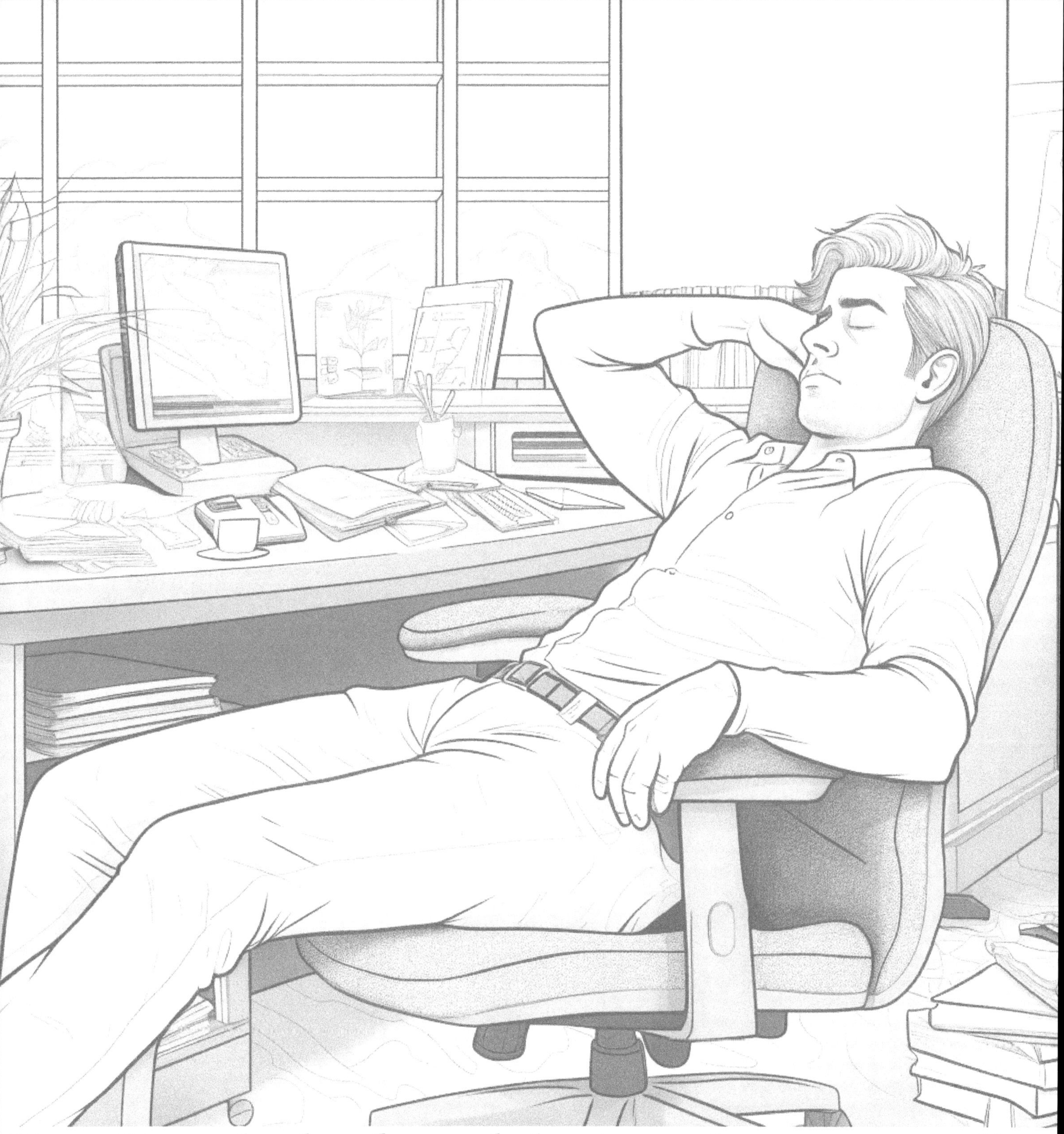

Unveiling the keyboard shortcut that trumps all: "Ctrl + Zzz," where computer updates magically trigger sleep mode.

Paperwork Pandemonium

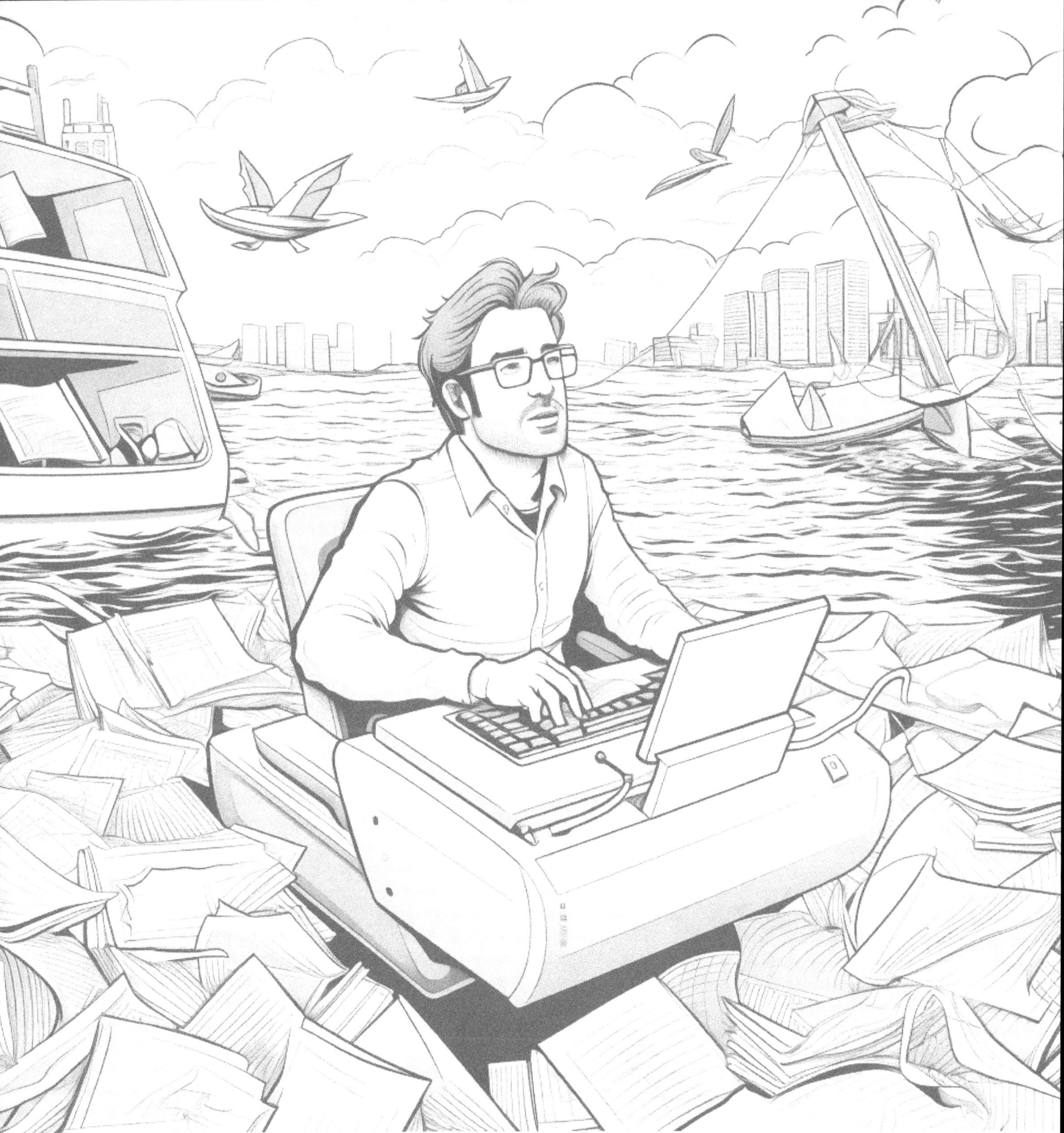

Drowning in a sea of forms, just like your motivation.

The Art of Escape

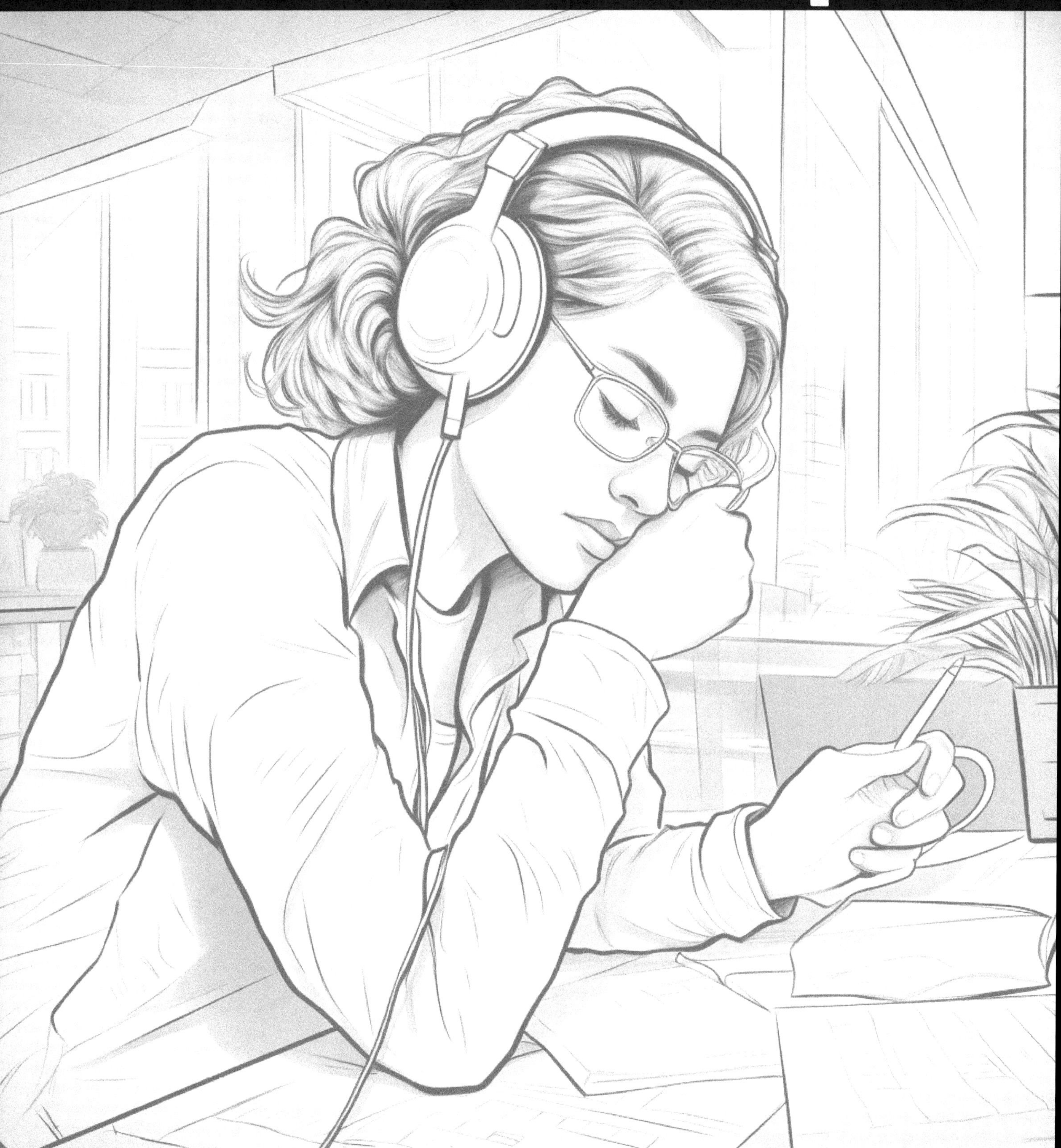

Doodling your dream vacation while escaping the grind - at least on paper.

Lunchroom Lore

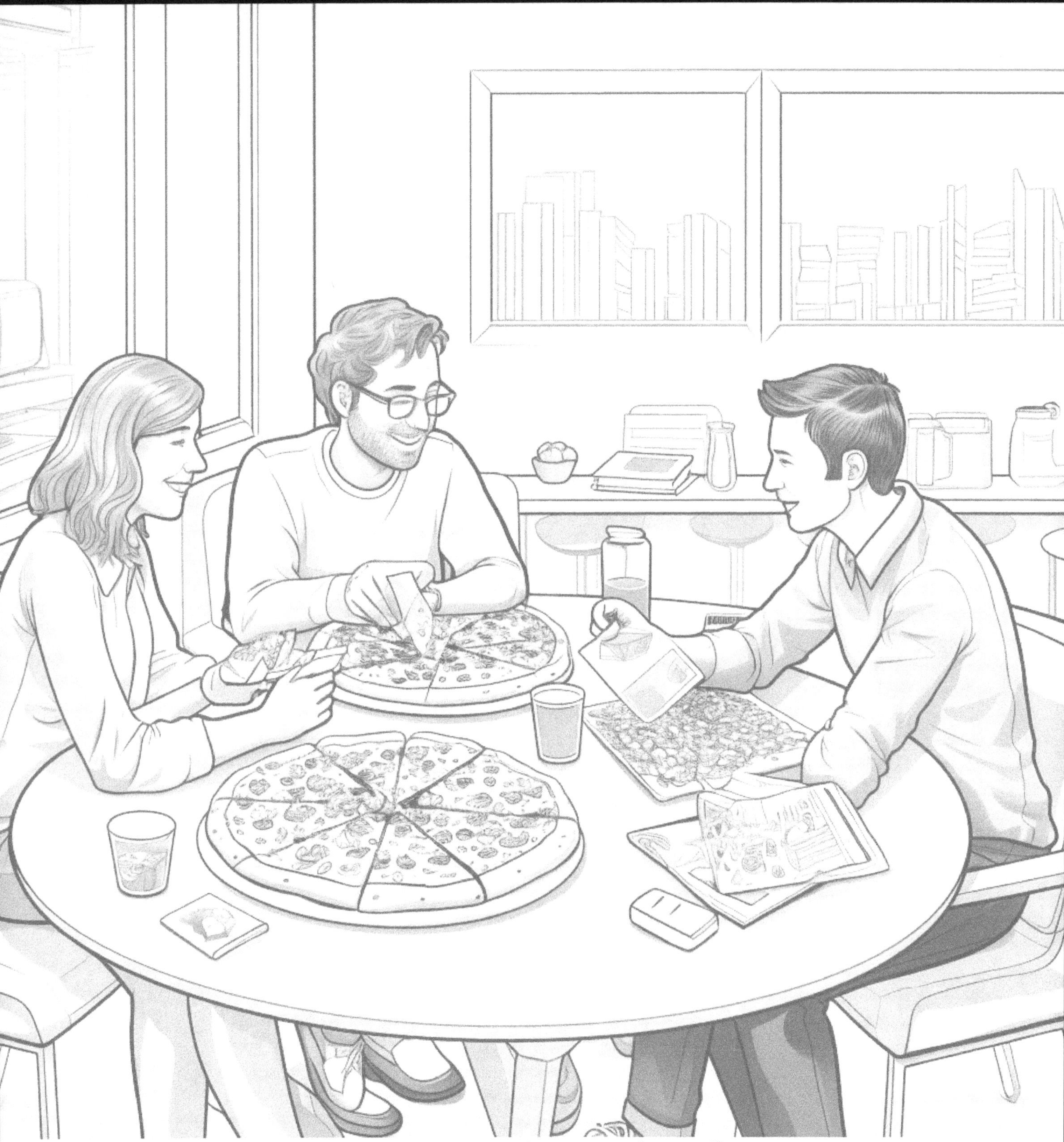

Listening to coworkers' life stories in the saga of the shared microwave.

Basket-case Leadership

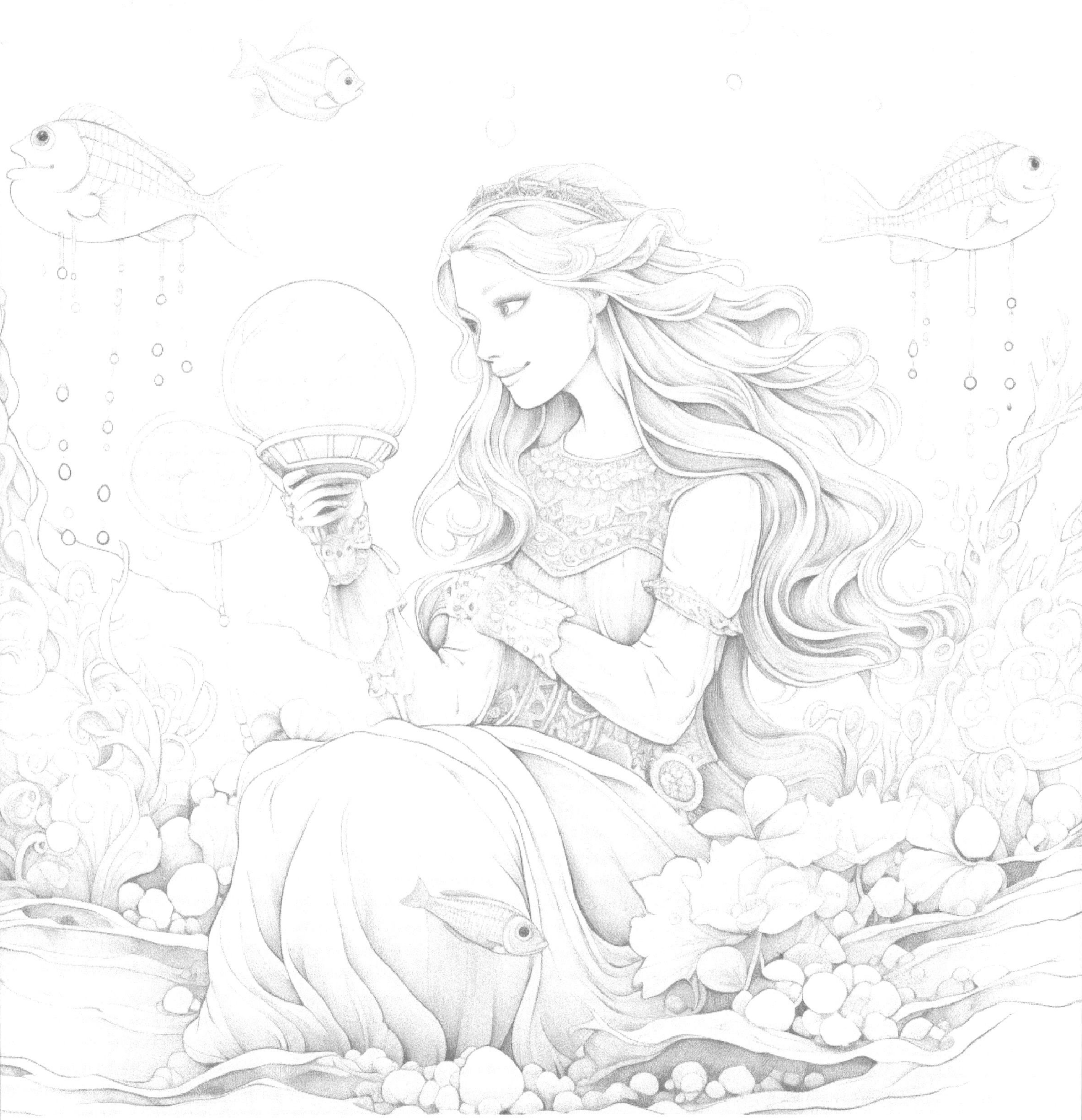

Embrace the expert guidance of a boss whose Master's Degree in Underwater Basket-Weaving has qualified them for leadership.

Water Cooler Wisdom

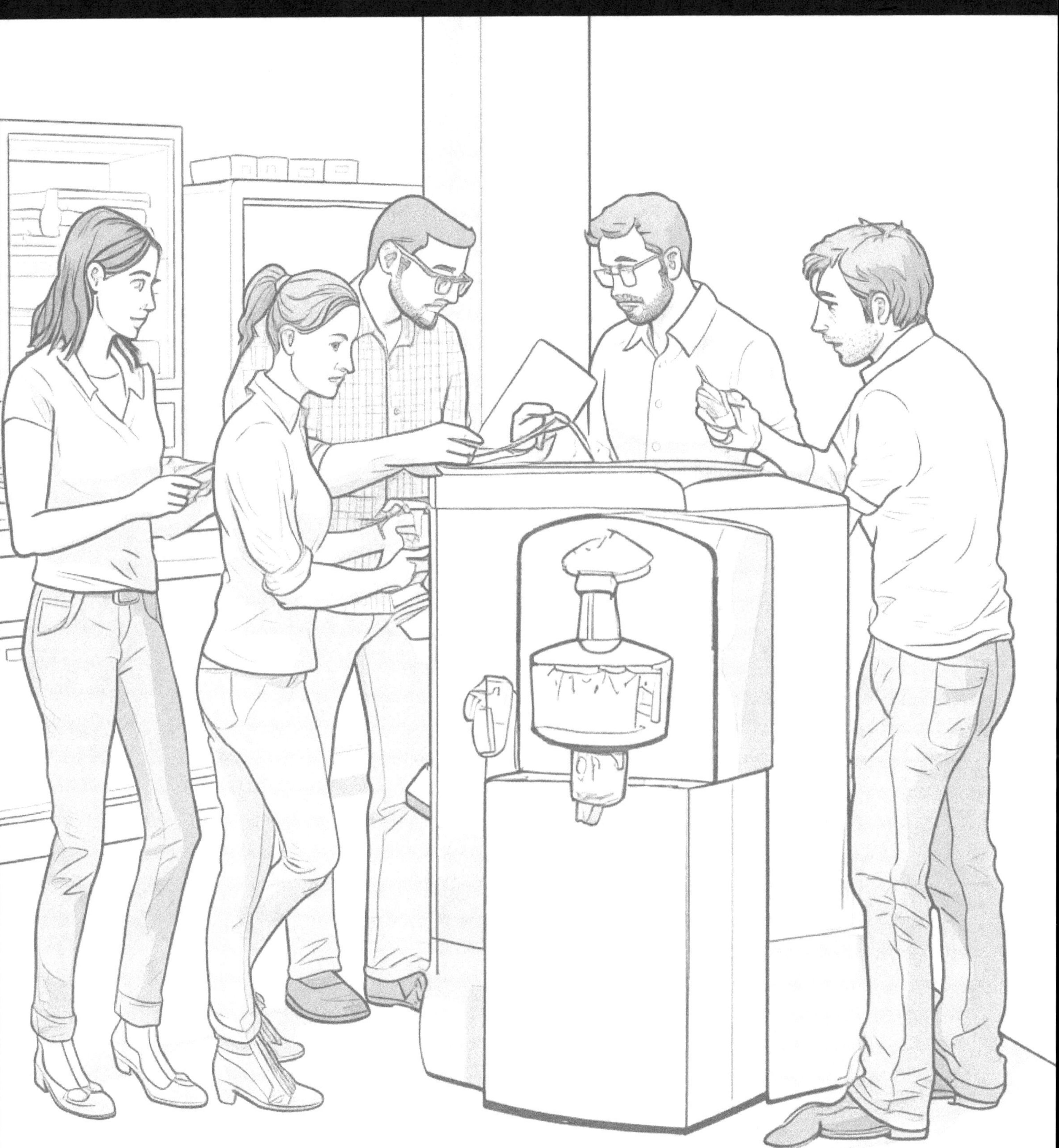

Gathering around the water cooler for existential conversations.

The Art of Pretending

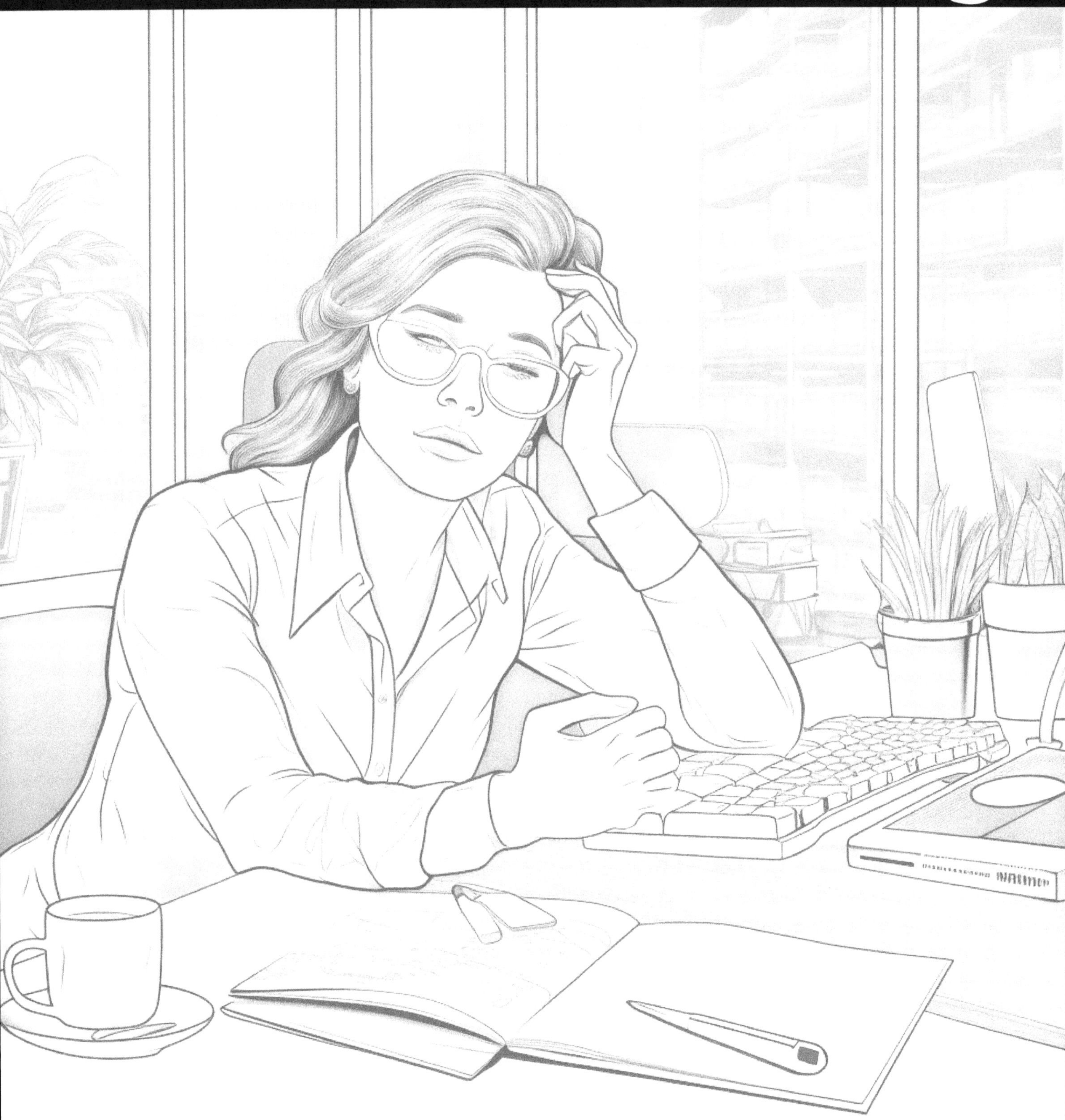

Mastering the skill of pretending to listen in 3...2... zzz.

Windowless Wonderland

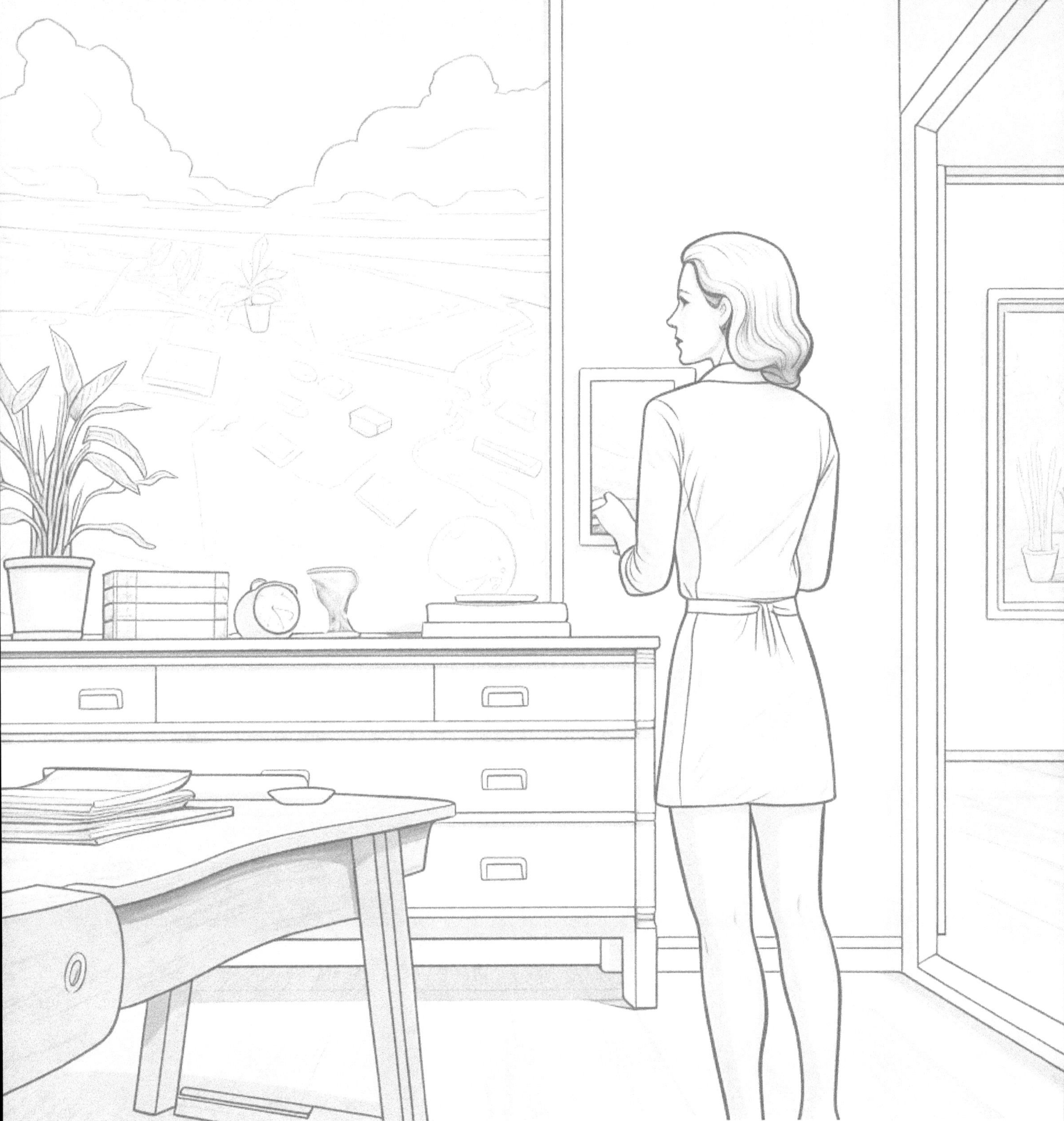

Finding solace in wall art, as the closest you get to nature is an artificial plant.

Meeting Marathons

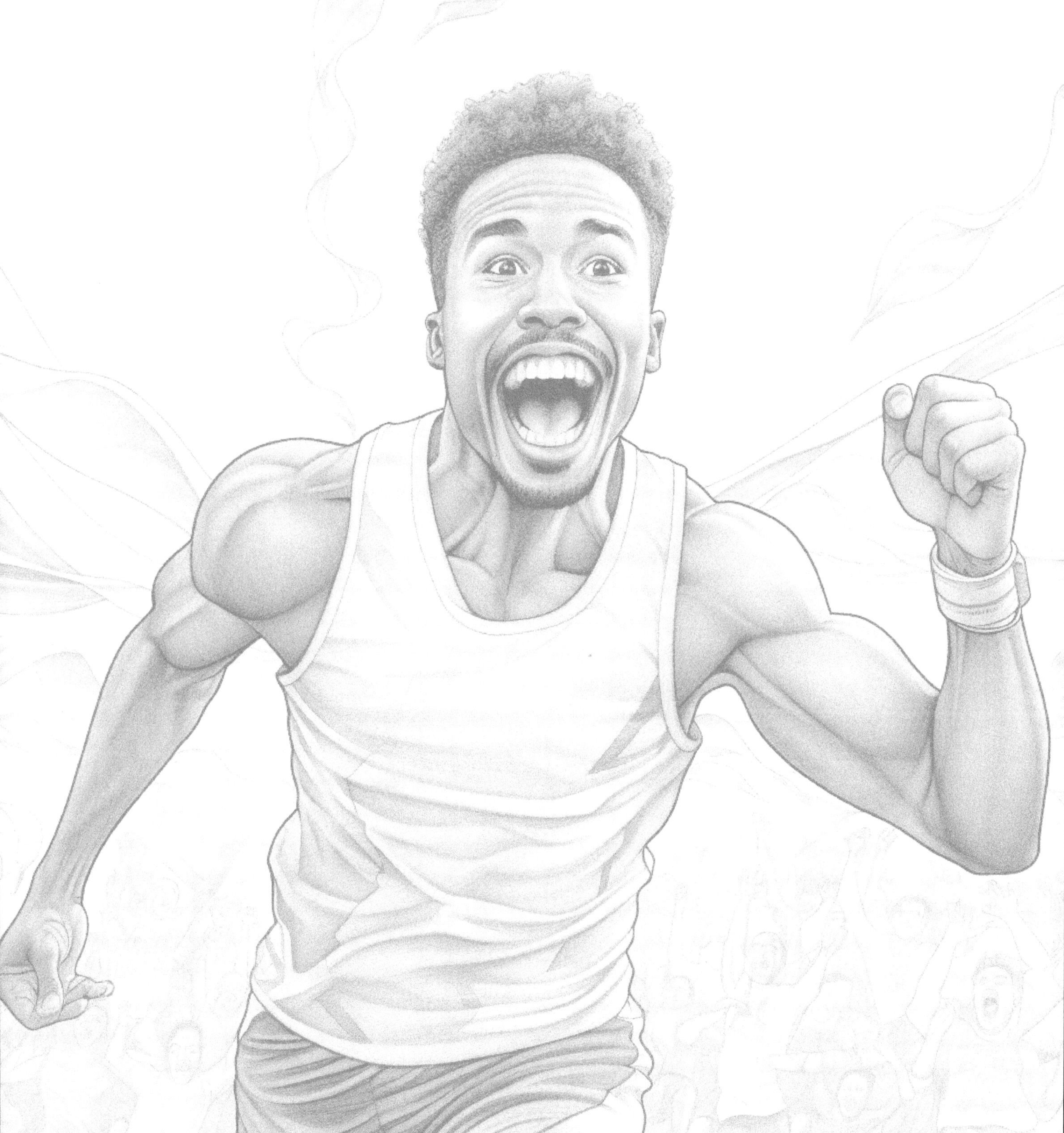

Surviving "Meeting Marathons" where the finish line seems to move farther away.

Inexpert Expertise

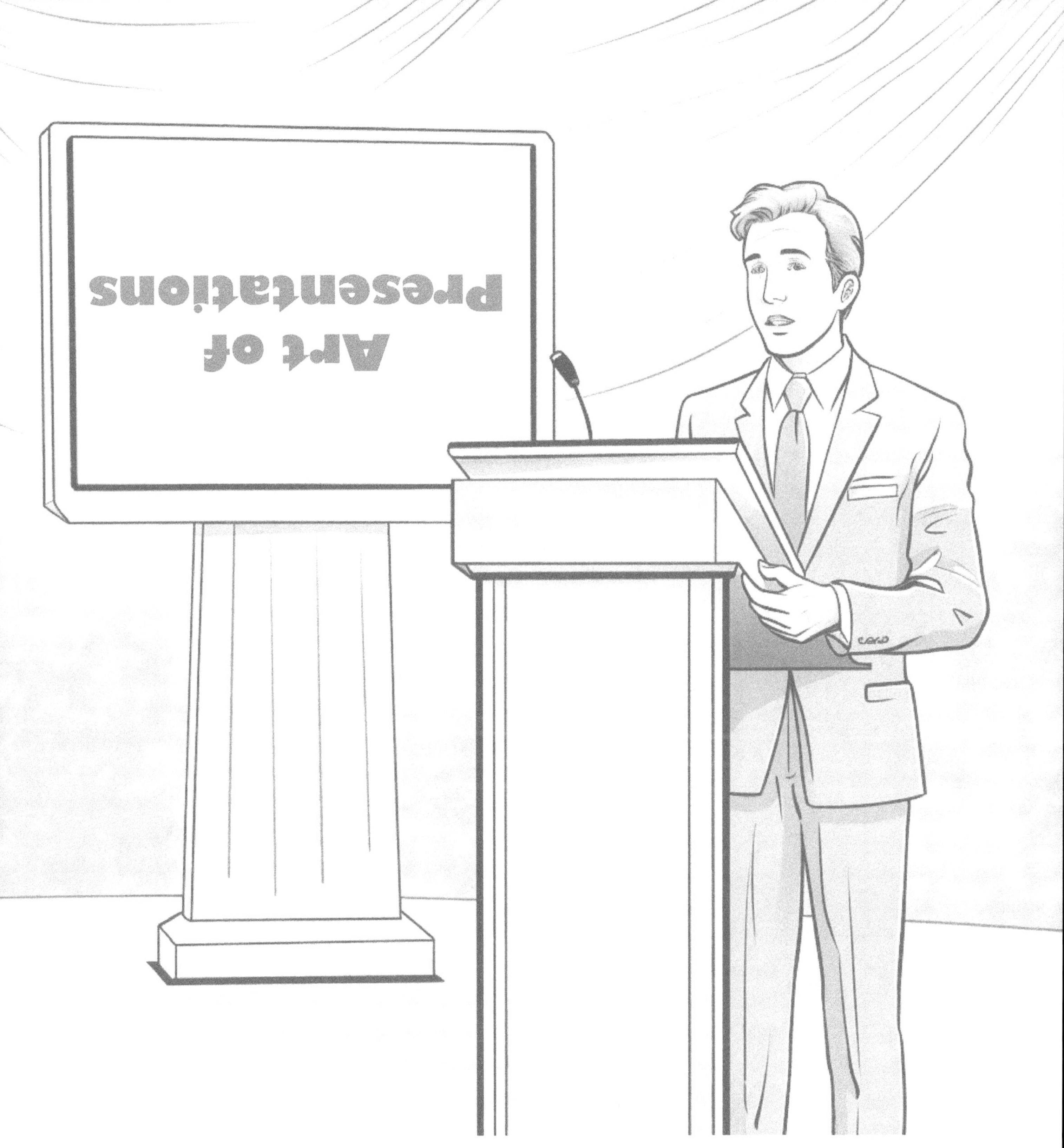

Experience the boss's incredible ability to impart expert advice on subjects they've never quite grasped.

Cubicle Escape Fantasies

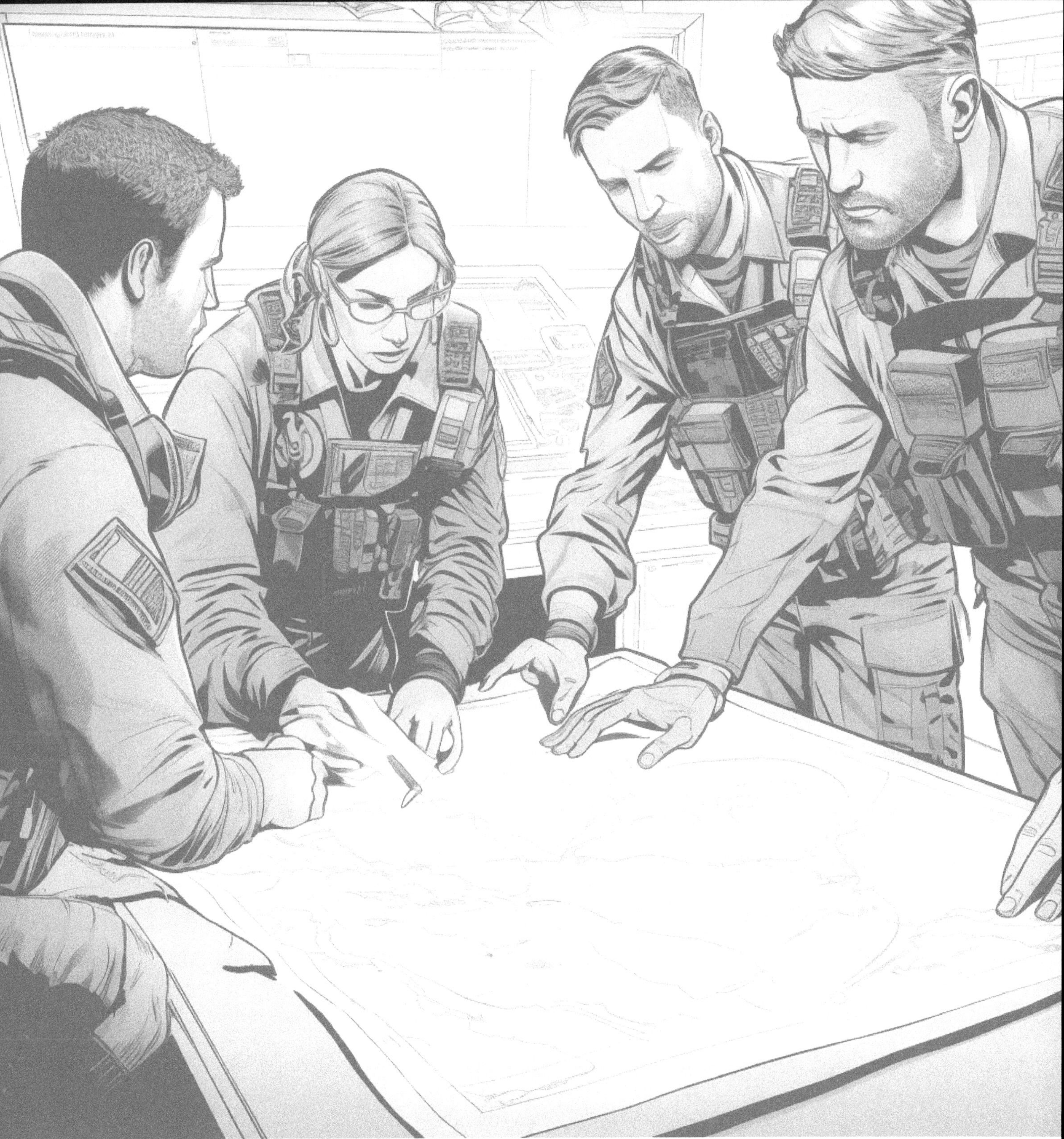

Embarking on grand adventures in your mind, far from the walls of your cubicle.

Keyboard Symphony

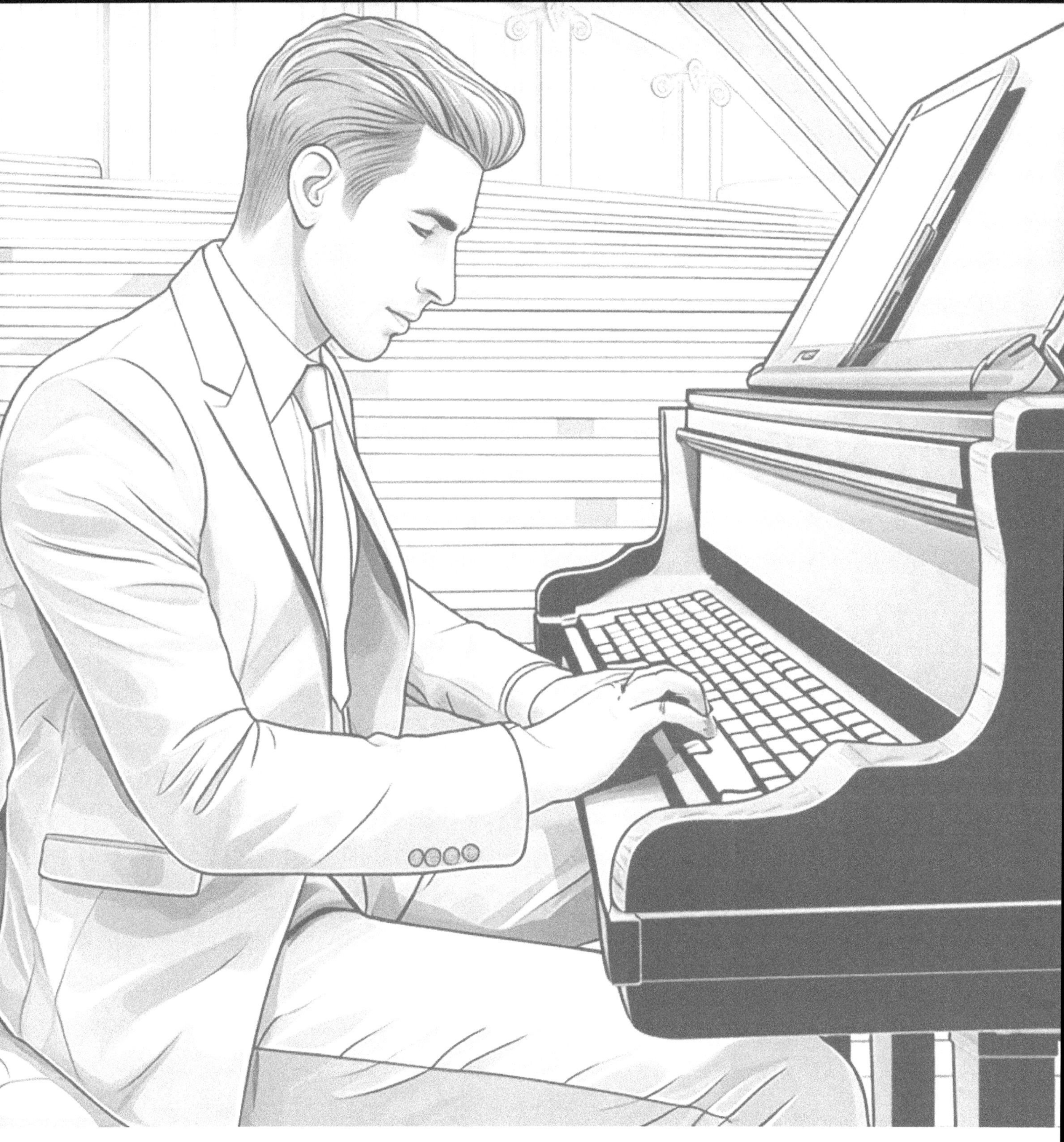

Composing a masterpiece with the rhythmic clacking of your keyboard.

Hangry Havoc

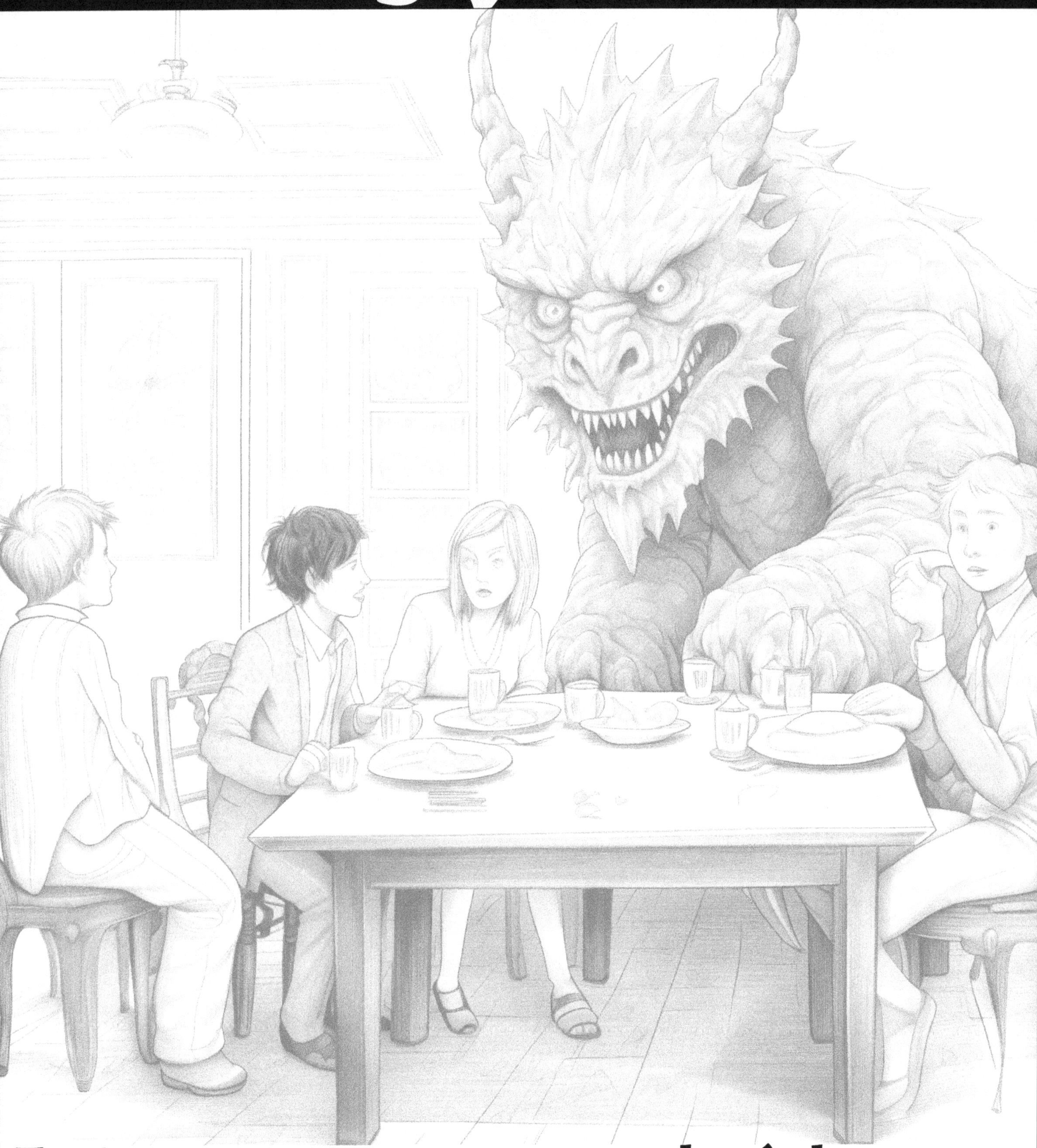

Trying to tame your coworker's hanger beast that arrives every day at noon.

Clock Watchers Club

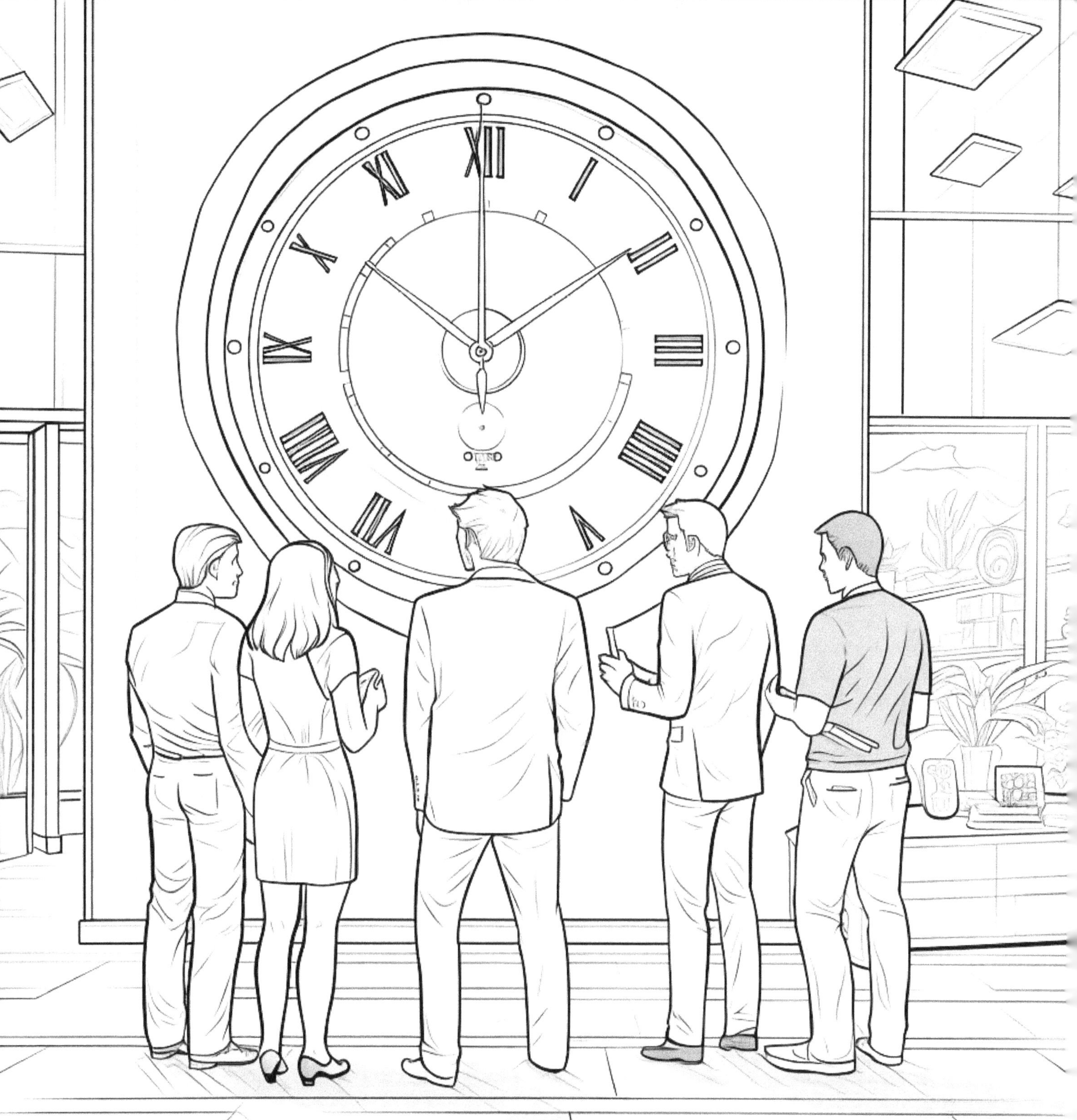

Officially joining the prestigious club of clock-watching enthusiasts.

Groundhog Desk

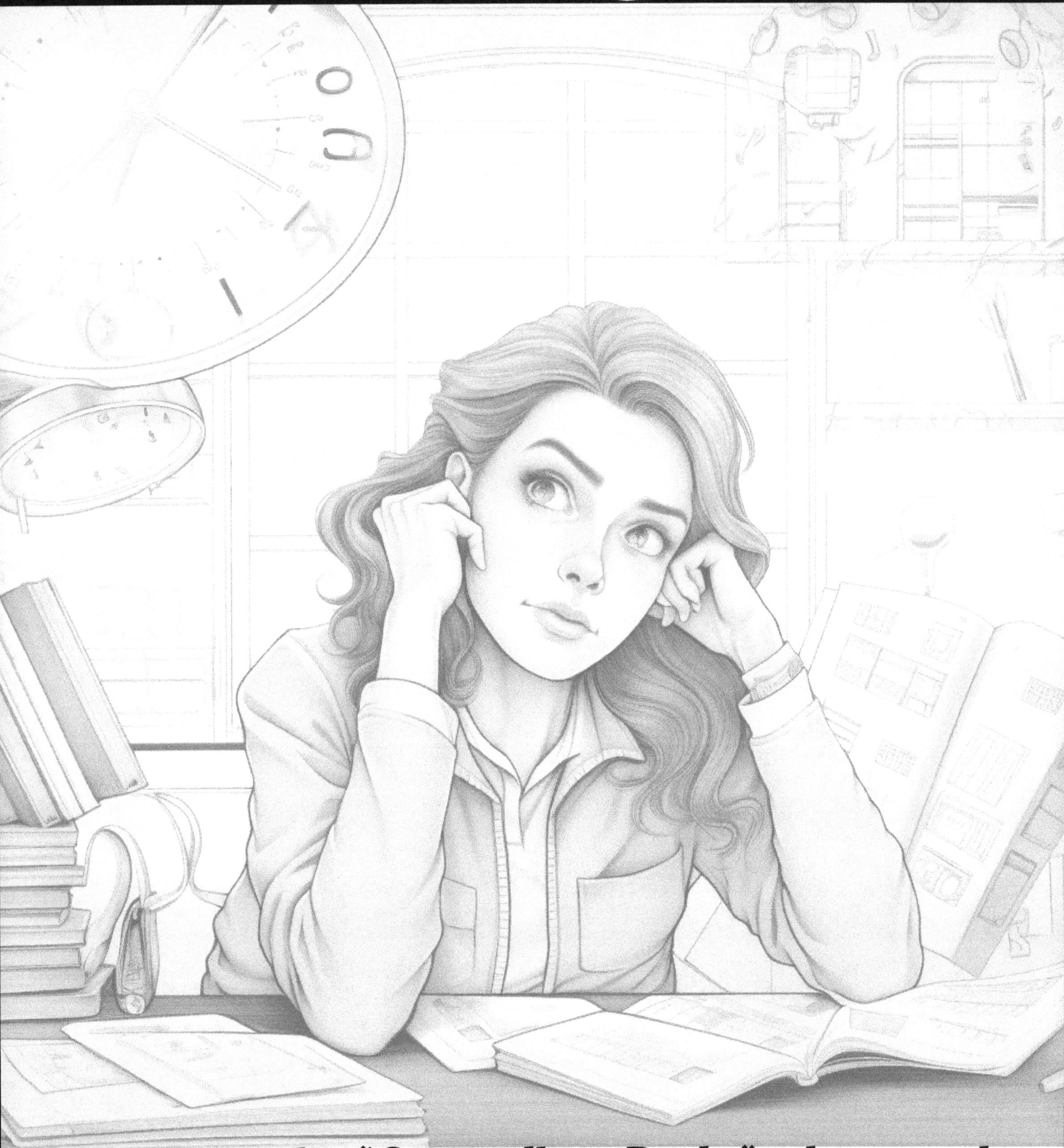

Experience the "Groundhog Desk," where each day feels like the one before, trapped in an endless loop.

Email Rabbit Hole

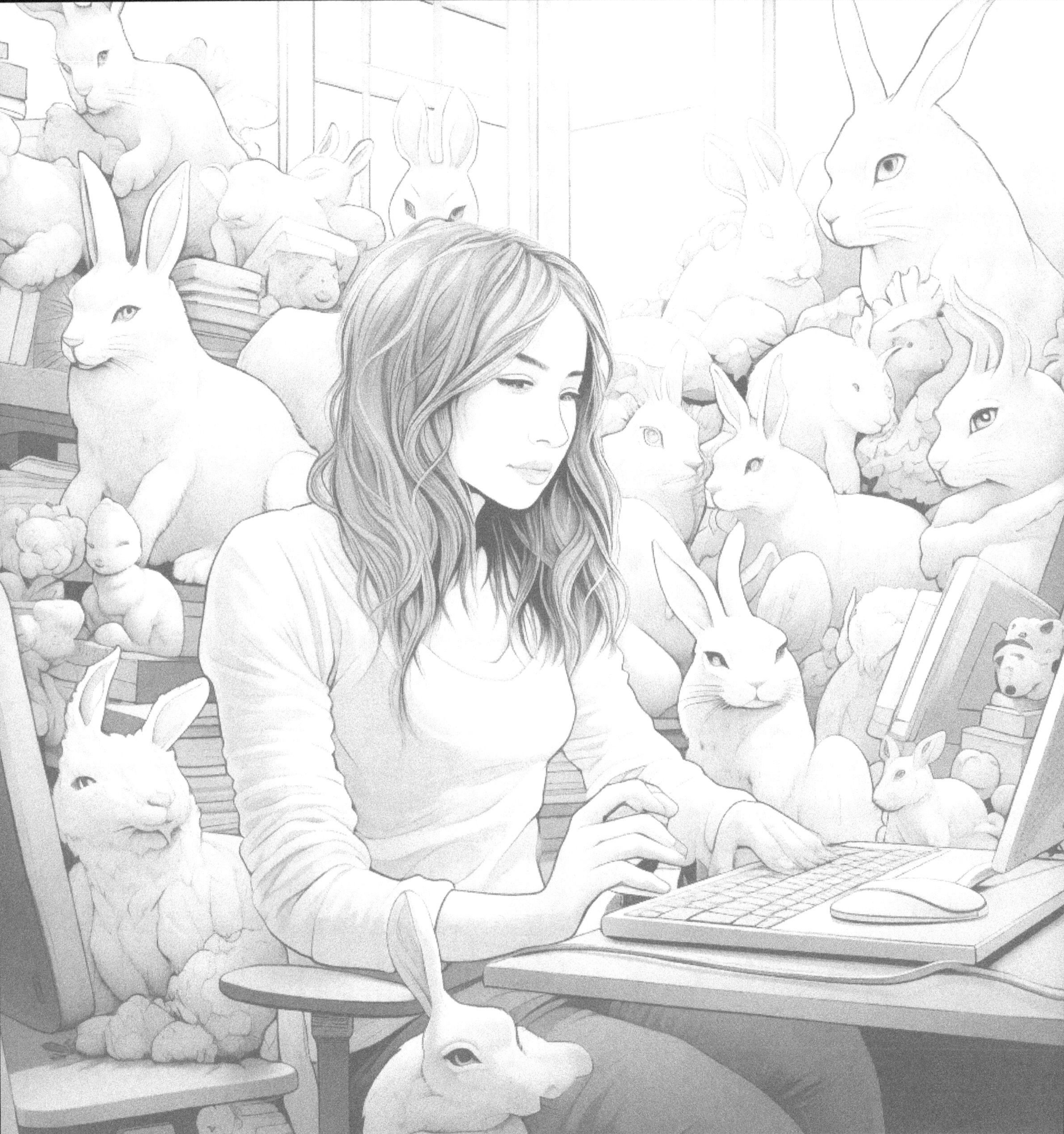

Diving into the endless abyss of emails that multiply like mutated rabbits.

Bosszilla Attacks

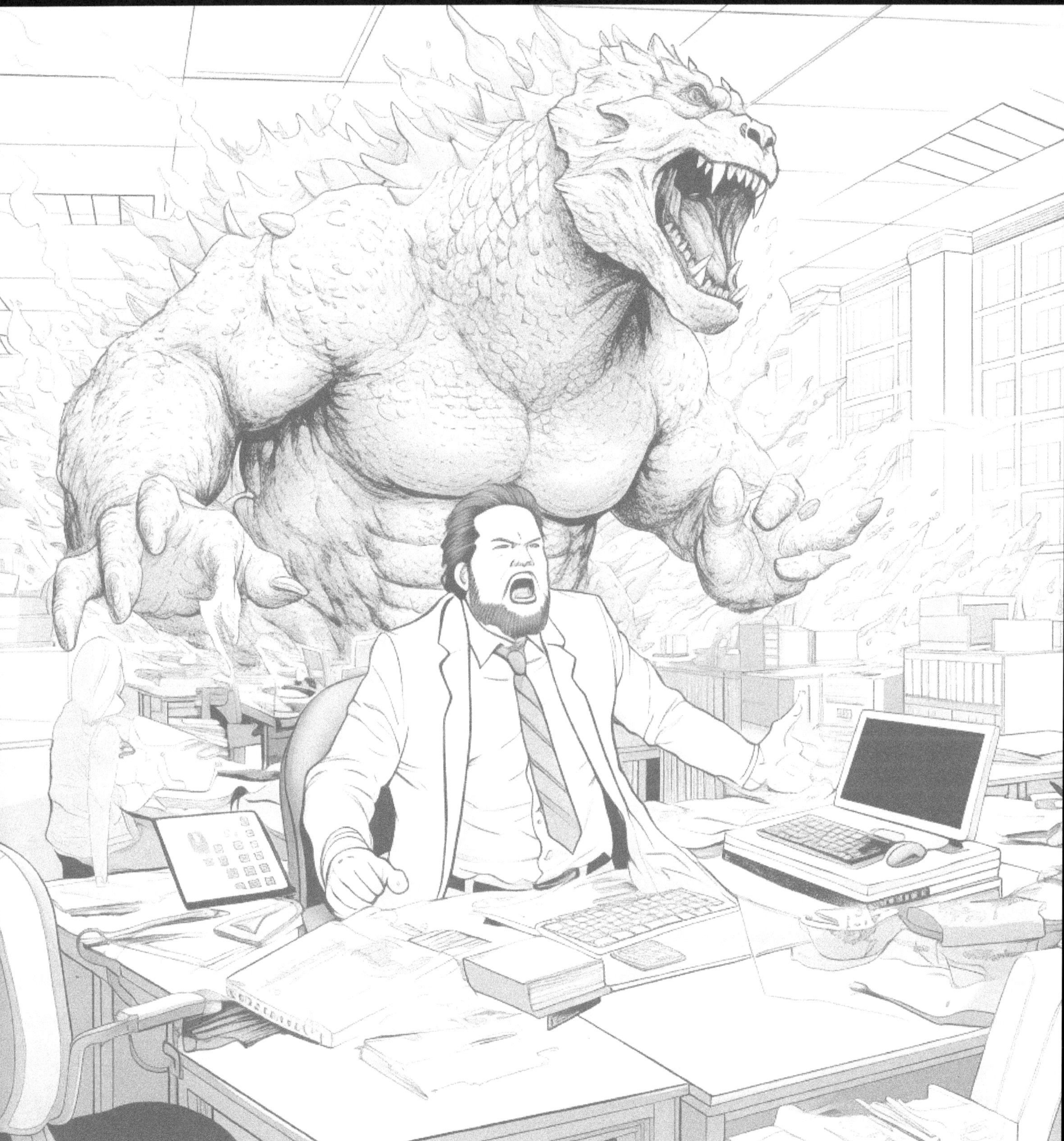

When your supervisor's mood swings could rival Godzilla's rampage.

Farewell, Toxicity!

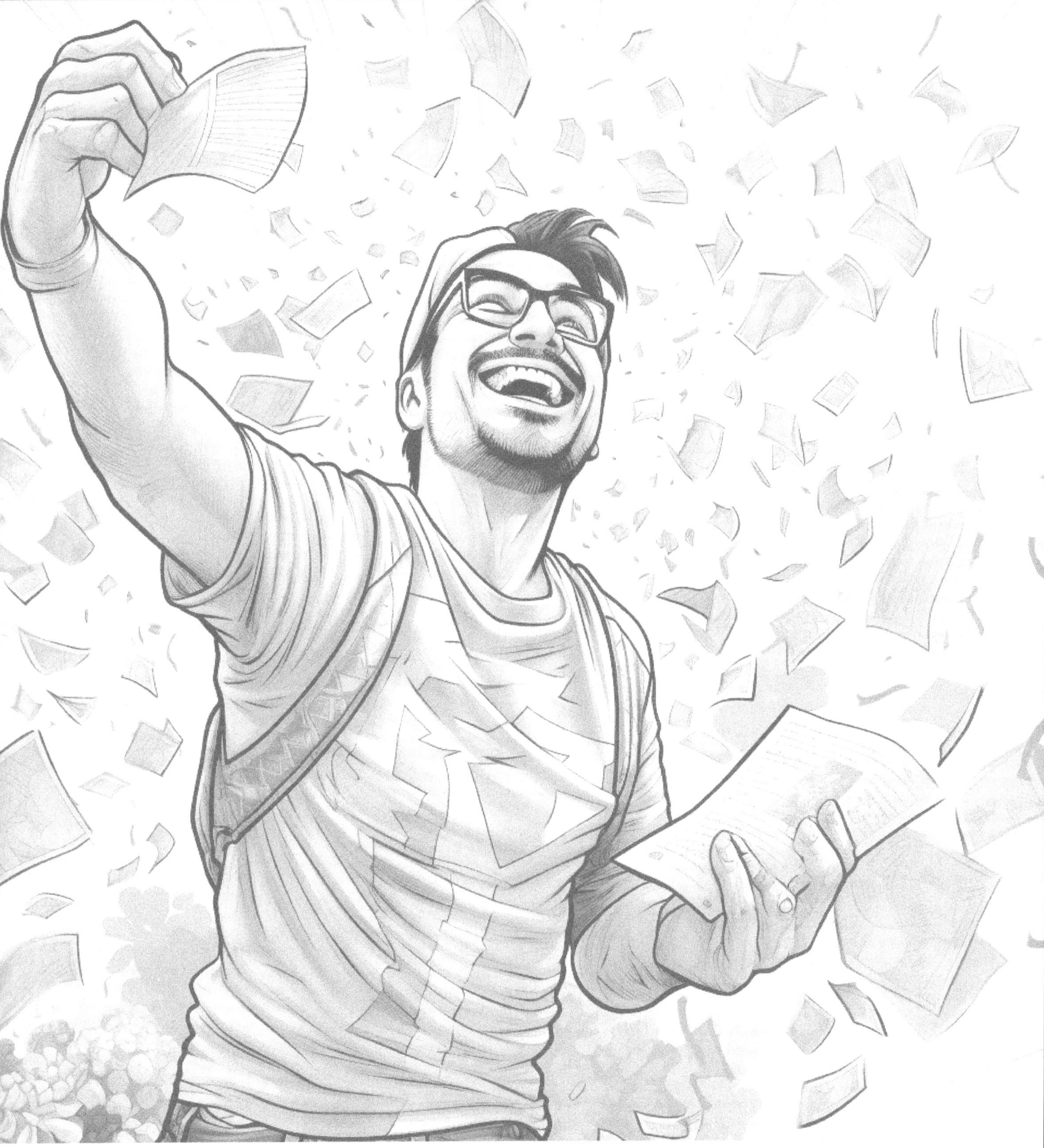

That beautiful day when you turn your resignation into a confetti filled fiesta!

Bad Boss Bingo

Terrible jobs have some things in common. Join with a few of your coworkers and mark off what you experience in any given week. First one to Bingo gets lunch paid by the group!

B	I	N	G	O
Micro-managing	Favoritism	Stealing credit	Inadequate training	Complaining about past
Discrimination	No feedback	Rigid rules	Inconsistent policy	Incompetent peer praised
Using made up rules	Blaming others	Freebie!	Beating a dead horse	Interrupted during meeting
Public humiliation	Fails to address real problem	Lacks empathy	Double standard	Ignores safety concern
Excludes from important decisions	Holds secret meetings	Withholds resources	No lunch	Lies about something small

Terrible Job Word Search

Make your meeting a little less awful. While they drone on, try to find these words below!

Words to find:

Boredom • Clique • Commute • Cubicle • Deadline • Demotion • Escape Firing • Gossip • Incompetence • Liar • Meeting • MentalHealth Micromanage • Monotony • Overtime • Politics • Prisoner • Promotion Rookie • Stress

```
I Z J I N C O M P E T E N C E D C Z H I
S B X X Q B O R E D O M C O M M U T E X
G F L Y T W T I K O C W W Y C W V G Z I
T E I Q P Q C P L X L O R G F U M P V L
T S A N A J I X A H W M O V D O U N D R
C C R G X O Q P P R I S O N E R E K M J
Q A M P P O L I T I C S K Y B M M V X K
N P W O I L J J A Q D E I G I M E V Y H
N E W M C U B I C L E A E T E P N J V P
J P T K D Z O Z U M J U R M Y E T O W E
S S T J E P B C O Y C E K A R S A Q S M
T F P F A O W P N K V T P S C P L M G S
R A K Q D Y U O S O T M R F L U H F O T
E R U W L F T V Q D C F O Q I D E I S U
S X E V I O E H W X D K M V Q R A R S V
S E P A N G D E M O T I O N U N L I I B
Y M Q O E Z L O Y Z L C T D E O T N P M
V L M H R L M L A O N P I Q R I H G R H
O W U F J W L Q M I C R O M A N A G E T
M M E E T I N G J F J T N C F B K G A A
```

Bad-Libs

Here's a fun story - have your coworker fill in the blanks and make this story your own ridiculous tale.

Once upon a(n) ___adjective___ sunny day at the office, I was ___verb (ing)___ diligently at my desk when I suddenly ___verb (-ed)___ and noticed something ___adjective___ unusual out of the corner of my ___body part___. To my surprise, I saw my coworker, ___coworker name___, in a very ___adjective___ situation.

There (he/she) was, ___verb (ing)___ with a ___noun___ in (his/her) hand, trying to ___verb___ it into the ___noun___ while ___verb (ing)___ loudly. It was as if (he/she) had no idea that anyone else was in the office!

My ___emotion___ started to ___verb___ a million miles an hour as I debated what to do. Should I ___verb___ out and pretend I didn't see anything? Or should I ___verb___ and offer a(n) ___adjective___ excuse for the unexpected ___noun___?

In the end, I chose to ___verb___ and ___adverb___ approach ___coworker___ and see if (he/she) needed any assistance. (He/She) looked up at me, ___emotion___, and ___verb (-ed)___ ___adverb___, saying, "I could use a hand here!"

We both ___verb -ed___ and had a ___adjective___ laugh about the situation, and it turned out that (he/she) was just ___verb (ing)___ some ___noun___ for a surprise office ___activity___ to celebrate our recent ___noun___. It was a memorable ___noun___ that we would ___verb___ about for years to come.

Scavenger Hunt

Need more ridiculous fun?

Try this scavenger hunt around the office. See who gets the most in one week. The prize? I don't know, bragging rights, I guess! Also, pics or it didn't happen!

See if you can find a(n)...

- Enthusiastic newbie - someone who's still smiling with no Rx
- Dress code rebel - skating up to the edge of the code
- Mystery stain in a break room
- The secret lair of the boss who's always missing
- A neurodivergent lunch (i.e. dino chicken nugs)
- Jenga desk with piles about to fall
- Time capsule - someone with an iPhone 6 series
- Quiet riot zone - employees gathering to vent
- Jam session - copier jamming
- Cone of silence - area where everyone only whispers
- Mystery smell source - find what's stinking up the fridge
- Office Supply Artist - making art of boring office stuff
- Office Ninja - moving stealthily and sneaking up on folks
- Computer that doesn't need restarting all week
- Office DJ - blasting music for everyone while working
- Sleeper cell - someone falling asleep at their desk
- Inspirational art work that inspires no one
- Loud office talker - in action assaulting some ears

Word Search
Answer Key

I Z J I N C O M P E T E N C E D C Z H I
S B X X Q B O R E D O M C O M M U T E X
G F L Y T W T I K O C W W Y C W V G Z I
T E I Q P Q C P L X L O R G F U M P V L
T S A N A J I X A H W M O V D O U N D R
C C R G X O Q P P R I S O N E R E K M J
Q A M P P O L I T I C S K Y B M M V X K
N P W O I L J J A Q D E I G I M E V Y H
N E W M C U B I C L E A E T E P N J V P
J P T K D Z O Z U M J U R M Y E T O W E
S S T J E P B C O Y C E K A R S A Q S M
T F P F A O W P N K V T P S C P L M G S
R A K Q D Y U O S O T M R F L U H F O T
E R U W L F T V Q D C F O Q I D E I S U
S X E V I O E H W X D K M V Q R A R S V
S E P A N G D E M O T I O N U N L I I B
Y M Q O E Z L O Y Z L C T D E O T N P M
V L M H R L M L A O N P I Q R I H G R H
O W U F J W L Q M I C R O M A N A G E T
M M E E T I N G J F J T N C F B K G A A

www.ingramcontent.com/pod-product-compliance
Lightning Source LLC
LaVergne TN
LVHW081417110826
845149LV00010B/1771

* 9 7 9 8 9 8 9 4 7 9 0 0 9 *